JOHN ANDREWS (editor)

Discovering Walks in Suffolk

SHIRE PUBLICATIONS LTD

Contents

1. Moulton 4
2. Mildenhall 7
3. Fornham St Martin 12
4. Bradfield St George 16
5. Hawkedon 20
6. Long Melford 24
7. Stowmarket 28
8. Needham Market 30
9. Kersey 32
10. Stratford St Mary 35
11. Chelmondiston 37
12. Stanton 39
13. Woodbridge 44
14. Framlingham 47
15. Leiston 53
16. Southwold 56
17. Wrentham 57
18. Carlton Colville 59
19. Oulton Broad 62

Index 64

The cover photograph of St James Green, Southwold, is by Jeffery W. Whitelaw. The maps are by Richard G. Holmes.

These walk descriptions are the work of members of the Suffolk Area, that is the county branch, of the Ramblers' Association. Its five local groups not only walk the paths and lanes but are continually involved in the process of protecting and watching over the rights of way.

Number 263 in the Discovering series. ISBN 0 85263 559 1.

Set in 9 on 9 point English Times by Permanent Typesetting & Printing Co Ltd, Hong Kong, and printed in Great Britain by C. I. Thomas & Sons (Haverfordwest) Ltd, Press Buildings, Merlins Bridge, Haverfordwest.

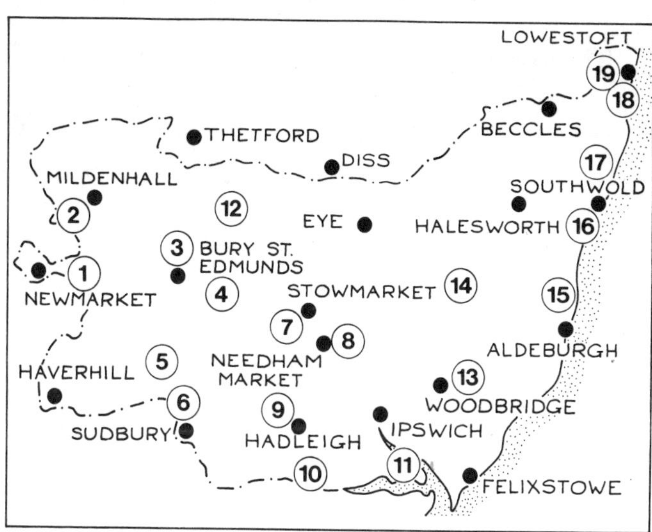

KEY TO SKETCH MAPS

✱	START OF WALK
	ROUTE OF WALK
(P)	CAR PARK
	ROAD
	TRACK
	OTHER FOOTPATHS
■	BUILDING
	CHURCH
P.O.	POST OFFICE
P.H.	PUBLIC HOUSE
	RIVER OR STREAM
	WATER FEATURE
	RAILWAY AND STATION
	BRIDGE
	WOODLAND

1. Moulton

Distance: about 7 miles.
Ordnance Survey maps: 1:50,000 sheets 154 and 155; 1:25,000 sheets TL66 and TL76.
Grid reference: 696644.

This walk is located in and around the valley of the tiny river Kennett in the chalk country at the western extremity of the county. It passes through two very picturesque villages and offers what are, in East Anglian terms, extensive views.

The village of Moulton, your starting point, lies about 3 miles to the east of Newmarket. There is ample parking space to be found by the village hall just down the road, called Bridge Street, which leads from the staggered crossroads towards Gazeley.

Return to the crossroads and turn right up the slope towards Kentford. When you reach the fork by the school on the outskirts of the village, keep to the right and walk along the good grass verge until the road bends to the left as it approaches a stream. Here a wooden footpath signpost indicates a grass path leading to the right, keeping along the west bank of the little river Kennett. Follow this path along the valley bottom and presently you pass the hedges and gardens of the houses on your right. Soon a splendid sight comes into view–a lovely four-arched packhorse bridge dating from the fifteenth century. The information plaque informs you that it stands on an old route from Cambridge to Bury St Edmunds; there must originally have been a far greater flow of water than the insignificant trickle now piped beneath it.

Turn left to cross the bridge and pause to admire the open expanse of the green in front of you. You then continue straight ahead up the Gazeley road. After a very short distance you come to a concrete lay-by in front of a waterworks pumping station. Here you must turn right along a concrete road. You pass a bungalow on the left and then cross the lower edge of a former vehicle scrapyard, where ancient cars and vans are scattered amongst the shrubs of the hillside. Keep straight on along the lower edge of a field and climb a series of three stiles. When you have negotiated the third you will be at the bottom end of an avenue of horse-chestnut trees which starts at the rear wall of the churchyard. Climb up between the trees and continue through the narrow belt of woodland at the top. You then emerge into a cultivated field. The official line of the path runs slightly to the right of the pole in the field, which is itself to the right of straight ahead. You have to head for the top right-hand corner of the field and pass through a gap in the hedge on the opposite side. You will possibly find that some path users have avoided the growing crops by going round the right side of this

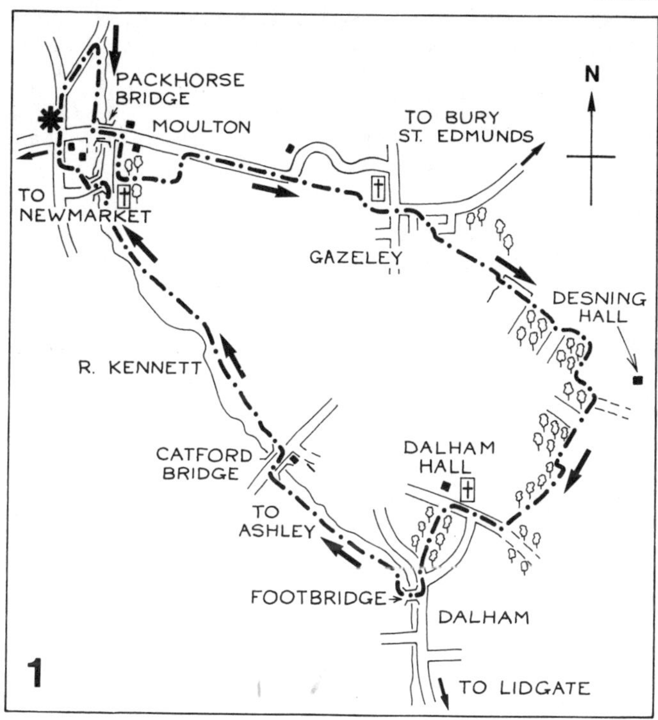

field. On a clear day the view to the north-west over the Cambridgeshire fens is quite impressive and it is usually possible to make out the massive bulk of Ely Cathedral dominating the skyline some fifteen miles away.

Having turned your back on the view and passed through the hedge gap, turn left and follow the left edge of the field back down to the road. Turn right towards Gazeley and continue along the road for some distance until it makes a ninety-degree turn to the left. You should continue straight ahead at first beside a field on the right and then along a path lined with hedges on both sides as far as Gazeley churchyard. When you leave the churchyard you have to cross the road and take the turning directly opposite leading towards Bury St Edmunds.

Almost immediately you come to a housing development called Tithe Close. Walk along a tarmac path that leads diagonally across the grassy space in front of you and turn right by number 22. Look for another path almost straight ahead between the gardens of numbers 25 and 26. When you reach the low stile in the hedge at the rear of the gardens, look towards an electricity pole in the hedge halfway to the left across the narrow field. Head for this and climb over another low stile in the gap beside it. Now your way lies straight ahead under overhead cables along a strip of grass separating the fields on either side until you reach the far ends of these fields.

At the time of writing the official line of the public footpath goes straight ahead here and follows the outside edge of the woods ahead of you along the northern and eastern side. However, an application has been made to create a diversion which would make the official route the pleasant woodland path around the inside edge of the wood which the owner has for some years invited walkers to use. To follow this route you should turn right for a few paces, then left over a brick culvert and walk towards the wood on the narrow grass path on the left edge of the field. Cross the wooden plank footbridge and go straight ahead through the wood. After a couple of hundred yards the path turns right towards a wide stretch of grass but quickly returns to its former direction. You continue past conifer plantations and turn first right, then left and then right again.

You pass next through gates to cross the end of another grassy 'ride' and after a last longer woodland stretch turn left to emerge finally from the woods. Turn right along a wide strip of grass down a gentle slope and then follow the path through a patch of woodland and finally alongside parkland railings until you come to a metalled road.

Turn right along the road, pass a turning downhill to the left, and go on until you come to Dalham church. This is a lovely spot; both the church and the hall, set back beyond its long walled garden, are superbly situated.

When you have rested awhile, look down the hill at the double avenue of chestnut trees leading down from the hall. The footpath leads between the trees on the left of the avenue; you reach it through a metal kissing gate and leave it by a similar wooden one.

Turn left along the attractive village street. Your route lies across a wooden footbridge over the river Kennett which is a few yards past a curious conical brick building on the right. Turn right at the end of the bridge and walk between the paddock fence and the riverbank. Very quickly you come into a large field and now follow the riverbank along this field and the next for some distance. Just after you come to a belt of trees you reach a road and turn right to cross the river. A few yards further on, opposite the imposing entrance drive to Dalham Hall, you turn left along a wide gravel road. The river is now a little distance to the left.

After you pass a small sewage works the track becomes a grassy one with hedges on both sides and then a narrower path between open fields leading along the valley bottom back towards Moulton. You pass through trees where the path lies close to the steeply sloping riverbank and then reach a metalled road at the entrance to the driveway to the church.

A few yards further on you should turn left to cross the river, either by the bridge or perhaps wetting your feet in the shallow ford. Walk along the narrow earth path along the left bank of the river until you reach another ancient, but much smaller bridge. At the bridge turn left and step over the low wooden fence. Turning slightly to the right, look for another low fence halfway across the meadows in front of you and when you reach this go on towards a thatched cottage, where a stile brings you to Moulton village street. A very short walk to the right along the street returns you to your starting point.

John Andrews

2. Mildenhall

Distance: about 13½ miles, but can be divided into two walks, one of just under 11 miles, and the other about 8 miles.
Ordnance Survey maps: 1:50,000 sheets 143, 154 and 155; 1:25,000 sheets TL66, TL67, TL76 and TL77.
Grid reference: 711746.

The walk starts from the market town of Mildenhall in the north-west of the county and goes beside the river Lark along the old Fenland shoreline. It then turns east and later passes through a nature reserve on a part of the sandy Breckland heath before returning beside the Lark again. In the latter half of some years the riverbank path described in part two becomes overgrown with nettles and can be a daunting prospect.

Part one

Start your walk from the market place in the High Street by the old market cross. Follow the flagged path along the northern edge of the churchyard past the large and lovely church and continue along Church Walk. Turn left at the end and go down a gravel track which bends to the right past old people's homes and leads along the lower edge of the playing fields of Riverside Middle School.

As you dip down at the end of the belt of trees on your left, you come close to the river Lark for a moment or two and then keep straight ahead along the 'tunnel' through the bushes that the bridleway becomes. When you pass the cottage at the end of this covered section, the path moves away from the river to the right across the fields and comes to the road at Wamil Hall. Go straight ahead past the entrance to the hall, whose facade presents a curious irregular appearance, and through a gateway which leads to a tarmac road.

Shortly this arrives at a cottage at King's Stanch, where you turn left towards the river. The official line of the path goes behind the cottage and down the far side, but in practice all walkers have for years used the path at the near side to reach the riverbank and turn on to the lawn to cross the footbridge over the old sluice. The former stanches consisted of wooden gates designed to keep a good depth of water in the river in the days when it was used for navigation.

Retrace your steps back upstream for a short distance to where a grass path goes across the field to your right. At the end of this you come into a green lane and, turning left, go round the bend into Church Lane on the outskirts of the village of Worlington. Turn into the churchyard and pass the south porch of the church to leave it by a wooden gate. The path turns right past a white-washed cottage and comes to an unmetalled lane, where you turn left and into another path along the edge of a newer graveyard, before entering the main street of the village.

Turn left and walk along to the junction by the Chequers, where you should turn right towards Red Lodge. At the end of a small bungalow development on the right, the road crosses the line of the long disappeared Mildenhall railway. Immediately past this you turn right along a sandy lane leading to the right of a red-brick house in spacious grounds. This lane, with its varying hedges and rows of pines, will be your companion now for 1½ miles. It is described by Shirley Toulson in her book about East Anglian trackways as part of an ancient highway called Ashwell Street. When you come to a T junction at the road from Red Lodge to Freckenham, continue along the road ahead towards Badlingham.

To find the next footpath you should turn left into the entrance to Blandings Farm, although you might like first to walk up to the bridge, which is on the Cambridgeshire county boundary, to have a look at the moated hall in its lovely grounds. Through the farmyard the path turns left behind the barn and then right again to go along the left edge of fields beside a hedge. Eventually you come to bungalows and gradually the track becomes a residential road leading to the Red Lodge inn, which has given the place its name.

Cross the A11 road with some caution and turn right for a short

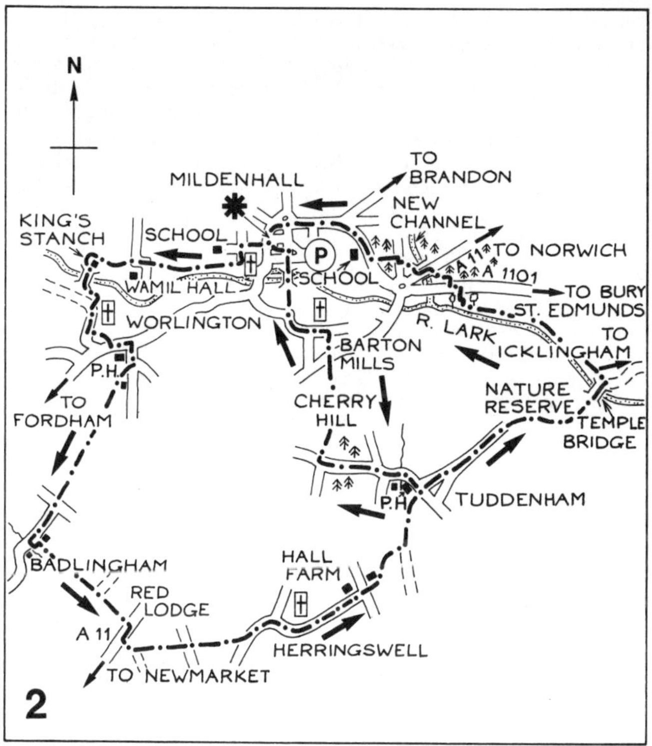

distance before turning off to the left along a wide cinder track. This leads to a scrapyard and is not an attractive spot and you will be happy to take the first turning to the left along a pleasanter earth road. You pass an area of grass and scrub on the right and then behind the gardens of new houses.

Crossing the next road, you go straight on along the right side of fields on an earth lane whose surface bears testimony to frequent use by horses. Passing through a wooded area, you come to a bend in the road leading towards the village of Herringswell and keep on in the same direction. At the junction by the war memorial, you turn right and walk up the village street, which is a cul-de-sac.

Beyond the houses of the village you walk onwards along the private road to Hall Farm and, on reaching the end of this, continue along an earth track which passes to the right of farm buildings into the open field. Quite soon it curves to the left and follows the field boundary into the far left corner, where you meet another track coming from the right. Turn left over a stile by a gate and make your way along a wide grassy track shaded by trees on both sides. Cross a bridge over a stream near farm buildings and follow the track between walls to come out opposite the large triangular green in the village of Tuddenham.

Perhaps a pause for refreshment at the nearby pub, down the road to the left, will help you to decide whether you can manage to complete the full walk or would prefer to take the more direct route back to Mildenhall. If you are prepared for the longer distance you should omit the next sections of the text and start again at the paragraph marked **X**. Otherwise, read on.

Turn left and walk along the street to leave the village. Pass the mill, now converted into a restaurant, and then the turning left to Herringswell. At the next junction, fork left and go gradually uphill, passing belts of firs on both sides, as far as the T junction. To the right an earth track is the only unmetalled road leading from the junction, and you should turn along this out on to Cherry Hill. Here the view over the village of Barton Mills towards the dominating church tower of Mildenhall and the air base beyond is remarkably extensive. Descend the hill and again exercise great care in crossing the A11. Walk along the road opposite and turn left along the street, passing the church and then the playing fields on the left.

The road bends to the right past this open grassed area and then makes a ninety-degree turn to the left. From this point the walker should be able to use a footpath not in existence at the time of writing.

The Forest Heath District Council, with grant aid from the Countryside Commission, is creating extensions to the rights of way along and near the river Lark at Mildenhall. The new path will be found leading straight ahead from the bend across the meadows to provide residents of Barton Mills with a shorter, pleasanter and safer walk to Mildenhall. It crosses the river on to the 'island', which is in reality a long stretch of land between the river and the millstream, and leaves it by another footbridge. Continuing straight ahead, you come up a short track to the town's car park. Cross the road in front of the car park and past the bank you enter the shopping precinct, at the far end of which is the market place.

Part two

From the market place head away from the High Street and the church and turn right through the shopping precinct at the end. When you come to King's Street opposite the car park, cross the road and then turn right before going left again up the road towards the swimming pool. Almost immediately you turn right with a smaller car park on your left to go down a newly created footpath to Barton Mills (see above). Crossing two footbridges and the meadows beyond, you come to a sharp bend in the road and go straight ahead up it.

Bear round to the left along the village street and pass the church before taking the next turning to the right, which leads to the A11. Once across this, go straight ahead along an earth road leading up to Cherry Hill, where it is worth taking a look behind you to admire the view. When you reach the road, turn left and go down the hill towards the village of Tuddenham. Join another road and pass a junction on the right and then walk into the village, passing the Mill Restaurant, to continue up the street and turn left when you come to the green.

X Go along the left side of the green, with its mixture of old and newer houses, and straight ahead along the quiet lane beyond. After some distance you pass the entrance to the nature reserve in Tuddenham Fen on the left and then the lane becomes a sandy track across a larger expanse of the nature reserve on Cavenham Heath. This is one of the few surviving areas of the Breckland heaths that has not been obliterated by forestry operations. It is a little difficult to believe that the route you are following was once the London to Norwich road and that Temple Bridge, though not the crude concrete structure which you soon cross, was probably the earliest bridging point over the river in this district.

This area of the river Lark valley has produced a great deal of evidence of Roman occupation and earlier civilisations, notably from the village of Icklingham ahead of you. Unless you have the time and energy to go up the lane to look at the village, however, you need to turn left over the bridge and follow the north bank along the former towpath of the Lark Navigation. You will accompany the river now for nearly 1½ miles; in summer the path tends to become rather overgrown and a stick may be useful to beat down the thicker patches of vegetation.

As you come to the end of a long straight stretch and approach a belt of woodland on the right, you should look for a sleeper footbridge over the marshy dyke below the bank on this side. Walk straight ahead from there to a deeper and wider drainage ditch and go left to another footbridge, before continuing along a winding woodland path.

When you reach the road (it is the A1101 from Bury St Edmunds to Mildenhall) turn left for about 40 yards and then cross carefully. From this point until you rejoin the Mildenhall road you will be walking along paths which are not rights of way but are used with the permission of the Forestry Commission.

As soon as you pass the wooden barrier poles, turn left and follow a grassy ride parallel to the road. When this ends you should keep ahead for a short distance on a narrow path until a belt of conifers on a bank blocks your way. Turn right here and follow a path leading straight ahead, with an old wire fence on your right, until you come to the A11 by the bridge over the Cut-off Channel.

Cross the road, then the bridge, and just past the end of the wire fence go through an unobtrusive gap in the trees on your right. Keep straight ahead through the trees for a short distance until you come to a well used path; turn left along this. It soon bends to the right and brings you to the Brandon road at the southern end of the picnic area. Cross this road also and then turn right for about 50 yards until you reach the barrier poles at the end of a forest ride. Turn left and walk along this; it takes you straight to the Mildenhall road, which you reach near the buildings of the town's Upper School.

Turn right and go past the school grounds on your way back to the town centre. Passing the cemetery, you come to a mini-roundabout and turn to the left to reach the market place again.

John Andrews

3. Fornham St Martin

Distance: about 11½ miles, but can be shortened to 8 miles.
Ordnance Survey maps: 1:50,000 sheet 155; 1:25,000 sheets TL86 and TL87.
Grid reference: 851672.

The ramble described here is more 'civilised' than many of the others in the book and also makes a little more use of metalled lanes. It does, however, offer a great variety of scene.

The starting point of your walk is in the village of Fornham St Martin, on the northern outskirts of Bury St Edmunds, on the A134 road to Thetford. In the main street by a telephone kiosk is the former school, a low flint-faced building which is now the village hall. Walk down the gravel road beside this and, when you come to the bottom, climb over a pair of stiles very close together and go round to the right beside the hedge through a grazing field of rather irregular shape and surface. Cross another stile at the end and go down a short ramp of concrete flags to the car park of the golf course that you will already have noticed. Keep along the right edge to the entrance and then cross the road to the club house. Bear a little to the left, then go on ahead with a chain-link fence on your right.

You now come on to the golf course and, where the fence ends, you should not go up the slope, but keep along the bottom edge of this, passing a tee and green on your right. The next landmark to look for is a wooden footbridge over the river Lark, a short

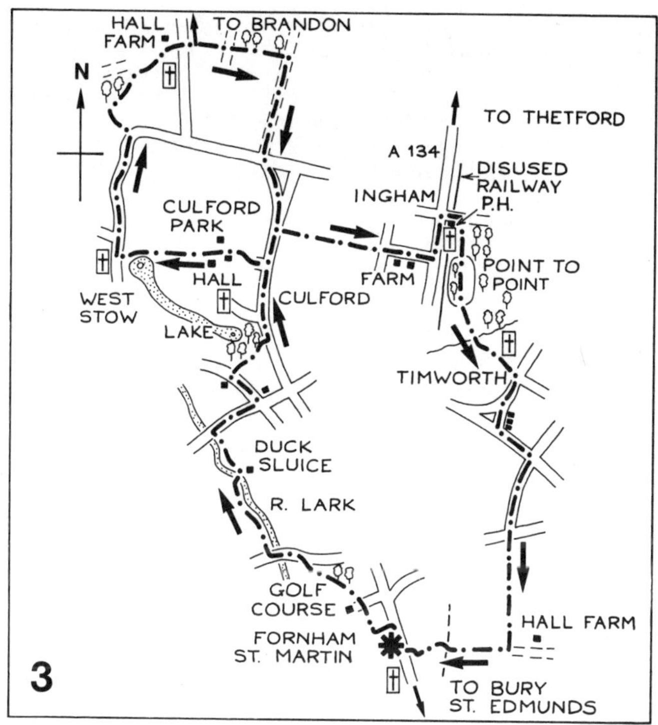

distance over the grass to your left, and, as you draw level with this, you should keep to the right of the next green and bunker. Passing another green, set back amongst the trees to your right, you now leave the golf course and go straight on along a grass track through the trees.

You come quickly to a gravel track, a red-roofed cottage and then a road. Turn left along this and go as far as the bridge across the river Lark. Footpath signposts point to left and right along its southern bank. You should cross the road and head away from the golf course along the former towpath of this quiet river. Only the brickwork of the derelict locks provides visible evidence that for many years this river was navigable and that barges used to make their way right up to Bury St Edmunds until the end of the nineteenth century.

Follow the west bank of the river for some distance until you come to a bridge across the river at Ducksluice Cottage, over one of the former locks. Cross the bridge, turn left along the side of the garden and continue beside the river. As soon as you start to go round the bend to the left you come to a wooded area and the path turns off to the right and goes straight along the right side of an area of damp grassland with well spaced trees, beside a hedge, to cut off the bend in the river. The fact that the path here is often wet and overgrown is probably why many walkers seem to keep to the riverbank.

Soon after the path rejoins the bank you reach the road at Hengrave Bridge, where you should turn right and continue as far as the crossroads. Turn left here and walk along the road until it bends left by a flint cottage and then turn off to the right along a track leading towards South Wood. When you reach the trees turn to the right and follow a narrow path along the edge of the wood close to the wooden fences of the adjacent stud fields. Eventually you come to the garden of a bungalow amongst the trees and, keeping along the right edge of the grass, arrive at the gateway of the entrance drive.

Cross the road and turn left towards the village of Culford. After you have passed a bridge over a stream go on up the long straight street, passing the massive wrought iron gates leading to Culford Hall; the drive is a public footpath as far as the church. Just before you reach the garage another less imposing gateway leads into the grounds of the hall, which is now a private school. The notice board includes the information that the road is also a public footpath to West Stow.

If you want to use the shorter walk, continue up the street to the entrance on the left to a house called Borderlands and look for the next reference to this in the text. Otherwise turn left and walk along the drive, passing the playing field and then beside a high wall, at the end of which you come to the main buildings. Follow the road past new classroom blocks on the right and then across the forecourt of the hall, built in the eighteenth century for the Marquis of Cornwallis. Carry on along the tarmac drive passing the cricket ground and pavilion and continue for some distance through the parkland. A long way beyond the school buildings you come to the northern end of a lake and then, when you have passed the overflow weir, you have to look to the right to find a small gateway leading to a narrow earth path which runs alongside the gardens of a small housing development.

On reaching the road opposite West Stow church, turn right and pass a bridge and some cottages by the T junction, where you must go straight on. About half a mile further on the road bends sharply to the right. In an opening to a field on the left, opposite the track to Brickfields Farm, is a footpath signpost.

Two paths start here. The one you want is not indicated by the signpost, which points to the right along the edge of the field. You have to make a crossing of the cultivated field. If there is no visible path, the line you follow is about ninety degrees to that of the signpost; aim for the left end of a small wood which stands back a little distance beyond the nearest trees. If you have found the right direction you will come to a stile in the fence on the opposite side and when you have crossed this turn right and keep along the edge of the next field.

After you have crossed a stream by a crumbling culvert bridge, you come to a gateway in the corner of the field and turn right. Keep along the edge of the wood and, when you leave it, make a diagonal crossing of the narrow field to continue alongside the stream until you come to another gateway and turn right along the track that you meet there. All across the horizon to your left are the conifer plantations of the Kings Forest, part of the Forestry Commission's enormous Thetford Forest.

Your route now approaches the tiny Wordwell church on a rise ahead, but before long it turns to the left and passes in front of the house at Wordwell Hall Farm. When you reach the top of the wide entrance drive go straight across the road and on up an open track across the fields. Where the track ends at a large field you have to go straight on over this making for the right side of the wood ahead of you. There is usually a narrow path trodden here, but, if not, you should find the correct line by keeping on alongside the wood and then straight on across another field to the right corner of a further wood, where you continue as before until you reach a wide sandy lane.

Turn right and walk down this and you will come to a road junction. Do not turn left towards Ingham but follow the road that goes half-left up the slope towards Culford. After the road bends right at another junction you go on for a short distance towards the village, until you are opposite an entrance in the low flint wall on the right which leads to a house called **Borderlands**.

Here you should see a footpath signpost pointing over a white-painted stile to a very narrow path between a chain-link fence and a tall conifer hedge. Walk along this and then go straight on, following a hedge which forms the right boundary of the field. Beyond the hedge the line continues directly onwards between open fields; it is sometimes ploughed up here and has to be retrodden. When you come to a T junction of concrete roads go straight on past farm buildings until you come to the main road through the village of Ingham.

Turn left and pass the church and school until you come to the crossroads by the Cadogan Arms, where you should turn right towards Ampton. You quickly cross a bridge over the route of the old railway, now disappeared, and have to turn right into the field just beyond here. The track across the grass leads to the Ampton racecourse although the official line of the footpath goes up the right side of the field. As you approach a group of trees, move away from the right side and cross the upper part of the course to go on downhill now with a line of trees spaced out on your immediate right. The row of trees bends slightly to the left as it finishes and you must follow this direction, crossing the circuit again and continuing down towards a shallow stream to find a footbridge. When you have crossed the stream turn left straightaway over a culvert.

You now have to cross a cultivated field by heading for a corner on the far side just to the right of the tower of Timworth church, which you will have seen partially concealed amongst the trees. When you have crossed the field keep to the right along its edge for a short distance until you come to the lane just in front of the churchyard gate.

This is a very peaceful and secluded spot; very little traffic disturbs the track down which you must walk away from the church. When you reach the metalled road at a T junction, turn right and walk through the hamlet of Timworth. Where the road bends to the right by a large triangular green, go straight on along the track on the left edge of the grass in front of the cottages. Turn left along the road on the far side and continue to a crossroads, where you should turn right.

When you come to a T junction cross the road and walk down an earth track between open fields. After a while this bridleway acquires a concrete surface and then, as you come level with the buildings of Hall Farm, you have to turn right along another concrete bridleway and walk back towards Fornham St Martin. A sharp turn first right and then left brings you into the main street near the church.

John Andrews

4. Bradfield St George

Distance: just over 8 miles.
Ordnance Survey maps: 1:50,000 sheet 155; 1:25,000 sheets TL95 and TL96.
Grid reference: 912593.

This is a ramble on the plateau of the clay country to the south-east of Bury St Edmunds. The area contains pleasant stretches of woodland, which are the remnants of the dense forests of early times, and a surprising number of well used field paths.

The scattered village of Bradfield St George is your starting point; there are places where cars may be parked in the street near the school or village hall.

Walk northwards along the street as far as a junction by a telephone kiosk and turn left towards Bury St Edmunds. Just past

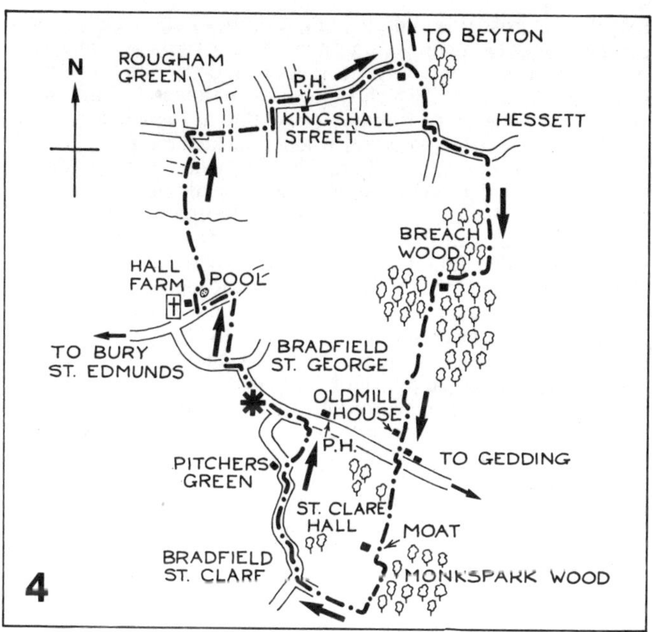

the third pair of houses on the right follow the line shown by a wooden footpath signpost, which points out a path running straight ahead by a ditch between open fields; it appears to receive as much use from cyclists as from pedestrians.

When you reach the next road, turn left towards the tower of the church, which has emerged from behind the intervening trees. Pass the garage at Bennicks Motors and Dairy Farm and then turn right through a gateway to walk up the entrance drive to Hall Farm. Continue past the square farmhouse and the farm buildings and at the end of the concrete yard you go through a gateway into a large field.

Bear round to the right past a cattle trough and a pool concealed amongst the bushes and, when the track you are on comes to a hedge, turn left with it to continue up the right side of the field. Keep ahead in this direction for some distance, ignoring the opportunities to go through the hedge into the fields on the right.

Where the grass track ends, keep straight on along a narrow strip of grass by a ditch on the right until you come to a stream and hedge across your line. Turn left for a few yards to a plank footbridge, cross this and go straight on beyond the hedge, now climbing slightly, again with a ditch on your right. At the end of the field you turn only a few degrees to the right and now walk along an earth track, which quite soon becomes a shady lane. When you come on to a road, follow this to the left for a very short distance to a T junction, where you turn right.

A similar short distance ahead, the road makes a ninety-degree turn to the left, but you must go straight on along an earth track past cottages. When you cross another footpath you go a few paces to the left and then right to revert to the former direction. The hedge at first follows to the left of the path, before changing sides as you pass a ditch pointing towards Rougham church. The hedge returns to the left before coming to an end and leaving you to approach the next road between open fields. You are now in the village of Kingshall Street, one of a number of settlements in the widely dispersed parish of Rougham. Turn left towards the junction in the village centre and then go right along the road towards Hessett.

When you have walked along this road for about a third of a mile you pass a turning right to Hessett but should keep on ahead towards Beyton. Along the next stretch of road are attractive houses, especially the black and white Pightle House. When the road takes a sharp turn to the left, just past farm buildings, you should turn off to the right along a grassy track with a hedge on the right, which immediately starts a long bend southwards. Follow this slightly sunken lane all the way to the road to Hessett. Here you turn left and very quickly turn to the right with the road and then left at the T junction just around the corner to approach the village.

Walk along a street with a varied selection of houses, passing a line of thatched cottages at right angles to the road, and just before you come to Heath Close turn off to the right by a footpath signpost pointing up an earth track. This track heads along the left side of a field towards the trees of Breach Wood, passing under cables and making a small detour right then left as it enters the wood.

You must continue along this track, which leads ahead just inside the wood boundary, for a little over half a mile, until you meet another track at a T junction. To the left it leads out of the wood, but you should turn right along a wider track which makes a slight but steady turn to the left. You cross another woodland path and then pass a well concealed pool on the left, before a red-brick farmhouse comes into view. Turn right here on a new track which immediately bears to the right in front of the buildings, passing a plantation of Christmas trees, to reach a T junction with a long straight gravel road.

Turn left towards a large clearing beside the farm; this is often filled with stacked logs. Do not follow the muddy lane as it bends to the right, but go straight ahead, passing a small compound surrounded by a wire mesh fence on your right, to enter a long field through a wide gateway. Make your way up the left side of this long tree-lined field. As you approach an isolated oak standing by a corner in the hedge to your right, make a diagonal crossing to pass between this and the hedge, using a just visible track across the grass, and then continue on this diagonal through a wider section of the field making for a gateway in the far right corner at the end of the wood.

Passing through this, keep on down the right side of a long triangular meadow to leave it through another gateway and cross a culvert bridge. About 100 yards further on, you go through a gap in the hedge on the right and continue straight ahead on a narrow but well used path along the left side of a large field. Follow a ditch as it bends right then left and you reach quite quickly a grass track across your route.

Turn left along this open lane, whose banks remain partially intact, and then, when you come to a belt of trees on the right, turn along the track beside them. This track dips to cross a small stream and then passes close by Oldmill House before reaching a road. Turn left for only a few paces and then right along an open grassy track; this route is believed to have been part of an ancient highway dating back at least to Roman times.

You pass a wood to the right and then an enclosed field before reaching the corner of the picturesque moat at St Clare Hall. Walk ahead beside the moat and when you reach the end you have to turn left and go straight across the cultivated field, the line of this often invisible path being almost exactly at ninety degrees to the direction you have been following. At the other side of the field you reach the boundary of Monks Park Wood. This and the neighbouring Felsham woods are of great interest to scientists and historians and somewhat unusual in that the practice of coppicing has continued there for a very long time.

Turn right along the edge of the field and, when you come to the end, go through a gap between the hedge and a tree and turn right to walk along the right edge of the field you have entered. On coming to the end of this field you turn a little to the right before continuing in the same direction between a paddock fence on the right and the field hedge now on your left. Making your way around the edge of the garage by a house you come into a residential cul-de-sac in the village of Bradfield St Clare.

Turn right at the end of this and walk out of the village along the winding lane back towards Bradfield St George. About half a mile past the water tower on the outskirts of the village, having followed the bends in the road to left and then to right again, you come to another bend to the left just past Pitchers Green Farm.

Before the road turns, a footpath, indicated by a wooden signpost, leads off to the right along a track over a ditch. This bends round to the right to meet the ditch again. Do not cross it here, but turn to the left and walk along a narrow strip of rough grass following the ditch on your right. You have to turn quite sharply back to the left as the ditch comes to the rear gardens of houses in the village and then right again to the road, which you reach over a sleeper footbridge. You have now only to walk along the road into the village to reach the point where your walk began.

John Andrews

5. Hawkedon

Distance: 9 miles.
Ordnance Survey maps: 1:50,000 sheet 155; 1:25,000 sheets TL75 and TL85.
Grid reference: 797529.

Your walk begins at a very attractive spot, the church at Hawkedon, which stands in splendid isolation in the centre of a large village green. Leave the village by the lower edge of the green and walk along the road going south-eastwards towards Boxted.

The road runs along the edge of a little valley for a short distance and then dips down to cross a stream by means of a bridge with white railings. You leave it to turn left up a track along the left side of a field. You quite quickly come to the lower end of a long meadow sloping up a shallow valley towards the small village of Somerton, whose church you can see on the skyline. Make your way up the middle of this and after you have gone about two-thirds of the way, to reach a point where the fence line on the left comes in closer, turn right to walk up a shallow depression, passing under overhead cables towards a stile in a corner of the right side of the meadow.

From the stile you may have to tread through the growing crops as the line of the path crosses the field directly ahead towards a house on the skyline. When you reach the now derelict house, go to the left of it, skirting the edge of the field, and pass behind the gardens of some bungalows. About 15 yards past the last fence, as you approach the churchyard, a gap in the hedge leads you over a sleeper footbridge to the right and into the village street in the small secluded village of Somerton.

Turn left and walk past the church and the other buildings in this peaceful place. At the end of the street the view opens out before you and you fork right down the metalled lane which leads to Francis Farm. As this turns left to approach the farm at the bottom of the slope you have to leave it by crossing a culvert bridge on a grassy track and then head steadily uphill. The track, with a bank and ditch on its left side, makes steadily towards the buildings of Manor Farm amongst the trees on the horizon. You approach the farm between a derelict red-brick house on the left (there are often donkeys around it now) and a barn on the right.

Your route turns sharply left and then right to pass between a wall of broken concrete slabs and a higher, older, flint wall. As it leaves the farmhouse, the track bends to the right and starts to go downhill. Just past the bend, through a gap in the trees on the left you should see two isolated trees standing almost in line in the middle of a field. These mark the direction you must follow by crossing the field, passing the first tree on your left and keeping the second to your right.

When you reach the corner of the hedge on the other side, alter course a few degrees to the right to continue beside a hedge along the right side of a field. Carry on in the same way through the next field and eventually you will reach a place where the hedge makes a ninety-degree turn away to the right. You, however, must go straight on across the field; there may well be a line marked out by tractor wheels. You quite quickly join another hedge coming up the slope from your right and, still following the same line, keep on until you come to the road from Brockley to Hartest, reaching it beside the garden of an isolated bungalow. Turn left and walk up the road towards Brockley Green. At the T junction by the green in the village turn left towards Rede and in a very few yards go right along a track towards the Six Bells.

Either this pub or the one at Rede may make a welcome stopping point, especially on a warm day. Your route continues beside the public house on an earth track which soon turns into a field on the right and you should here continue straight ahead along the left side of the field. When it leaves the field the path runs for a short space beside a ditch between open fields and then comes into the shelter of a high hedge on the left. It now becomes a grassy track which leads gently downhill, growing gradually wider until it opens out into Brockley churchyard.

Go past the south porch of the church, an interesting mixture of wood, stone, brick and flint, and follow the path to the left away from the church beside an impressive moat. At the churchyard gate turn right away from the large farmhouse set back amongst the trees and come down to a metalled road, where you turn left towards the farm buildings. Passing between these, with the double Dutch barn on your right, you come on to a concrete road surface and go up a slight steady rise. Through a gateway on the right you soon see grassy meadows sloping down to a shallow valley.

The track now acquires a gravel surface just before you pass a cottage on the right. You are now walking on a fairly high ridge with open views all around. The track bears left to arrive at an old farm, where you may find a number of coaches parked. Turn right in front of the shed with a red pantile roof and follow a narrow grass path along the left side of the field. Turn left through the gateway at the end and follow the right side of another field for just a few yards as it bends round into a corner, and then go straight on ahead along a wider grass strip running ahead between open fields towards the houses at Rede. The path soon joins a ditch on the left, passes under cables and then changes to the other side of the ditch.

You reach the road at Rede by a bungalow on your left. Immediately opposite the bungalow drive, a high stile with no step leads into a large paddock. Walk along the right side of the paddock and leave it at the far right corner through first wooden and then metal parallel bars.

Turn left towards the Plough and on leaving or passing it go left again down an earth lane. Continue straight on into the field, where the track leads down the right side until you come to a T junction with another track, where you must turn right away from the nearby farm.

Walk now along an earth track, soon joined by a ditch on the right, between open fields, heading for woods in the near distance. When you reach the wood go straight ahead inside its right-hand edge. Shortly after you emerge from the trees, the surface of the track peters out and you have to follow the edge of the field with another wood now on your right and then turn left to cross the far end of the field. From this far corner you will find a narrow path winding on ahead over a patch of very bumpy ground. When you come to a stretch of concrete, evidence of an old wartime airfield here, turn right through a wide gateway and then go left round the side of the field, passing a large thicket of trees, to reach a metalled road.

You are now at what is, in Suffolk terms, a very high point, possibly the highest in the county. Turn left and walk down the long straight stretch towards Gatesbury's Farm. Where the concrete road turns left to the farm, go straight on along a grassy tree-lined lane, which bears to the left and then to the right, coming out into the open as it reaches the southern side of the farm. There are open views now: you may make out the tower of Stansfield church in the distance ahead of you just below the horizon.

The surface of the green lane disappears but you soon come down to a wooden gate in a hedge, through which you must pass. Once through this, you follow a grassy track which bends to the left and then turns right to descend beside a long and rather spectacular 'staircase' of fish pools.

On reaching the lowest pool walk to the right around its further

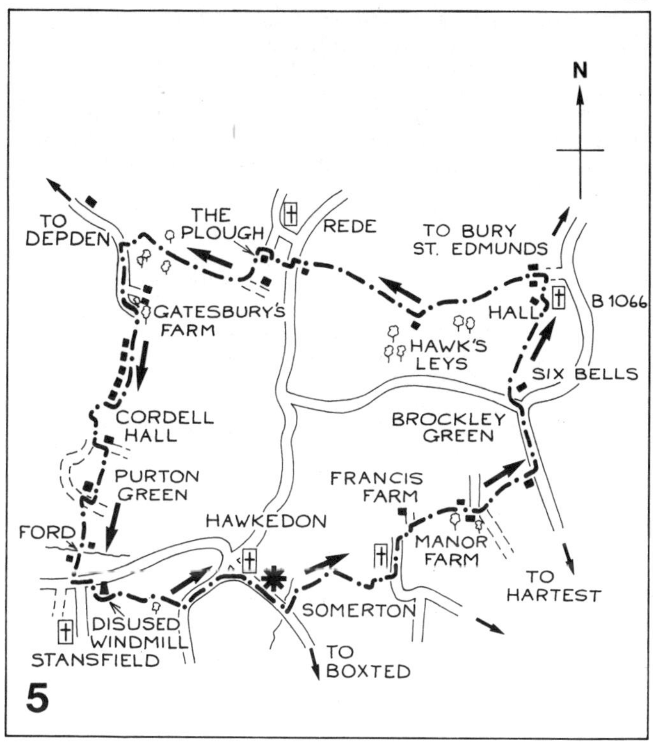

edge and then go down through a space in the hedge. Turn left between some scattered conifers and after a few yards you come on to a grass track. Turn right up this towards a clump of trees and then left to cross a stream close to this clump. Almost straightaway you turn left again and come on to an earth lane with trees on the right and then on the left. Pass one entrance on the left, but, when you come to the second, turn left down the concrete road in front of the impressive half-timbered Cordell Hall. Opposite the hall turn into a long meadow and follow a faintly discernible track down the centre. You should make for an old half-timbered farmhouse which is visible to the right of the far end of this lovely stretch of grass. To reach it, however, you leave the meadow by a stile and footbridge which are at the right end of a row of trees across your path. You then cross a patch of rough ground, aiming just to the left of the farmhouse. Purton Green farmhouse is an unusual survival dating from the thirteenth century and has been restored recently.

Turn right past the farm buildings and then left to follow a good narrow path down the left edge of a large field. Go through the white gate at the bottom by some cottages and then keep to the left when the path divides or you may find yourself wading through a ford instead of using the footbridge hidden in a 'tunnel' of bushes beside it.

Go on up the track and come to the road near Stansfield church, where you must turn left to the road junction. Turn left towards Hawkedon, but almost immediately go right up the drive to Mill House, which stands beside the brick tower which is all that remains of the windmill. The official right of way goes through the garden, but most walkers skirt the garden by following the left edge of the field. Keep on beside the field beyond the house until you reach a point where the hedge makes a ninety-degree turn to the right. Go straight on through a narrow opening in the hedge and cross a small stretch of cultivated field towards the corner of the hedge ahead of you.

At this right-angle corner you need again to go through the hedge so as to follow in the same direction along the upper edge of the next field with the hedge on your right. Soon the hedge gives way to a wood and then beyond the wood you will probably find a path trodden across the open field to reach a road at the crest of a low hill. Turn left and walk down the lane towards Hawkedon church, which you will have been able to see for some time already.

John Andrews

6. Long Melford

Distance: about 8½ miles.
Ordnance Survey maps: 1:50,000 sheet 155; 1:25,000 sheet TL84.
Grid reference: 865465.

This walk allows you to see some of East Anglia's loveliest buildings in and around the fascinating village of Long Melford.

Start your walk near the road junction at the upper end of the Green in Long Melford and go up the short road beside the Black Lion hotel to the church, one of the most magnificent parish churches in England. Leave the churchyard by the gateway which is opposite the west door at the base of the tower. Go straight ahead for about 50 yards, pass the entrance to the rectory on your right and then turn right over a stile and walk along the edge of the paddock beside the garden fence. Cross another stile to leave the paddock and then a third one about 25 yards further on.

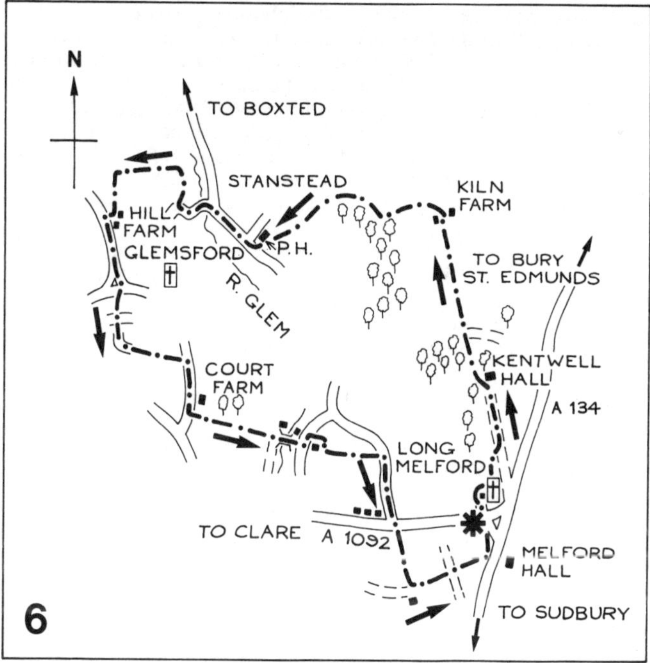

From this point the red-brick buildings of Kentwell Hall can be seen far ahead at the end of a long expanse of grass. You should walk directly towards the hall for about 175 yards, following a barely visible depression on the grass, and then turn half to the right along another depression even more difficult to make out. If you are on the right line you will shortly reach the drive to the hall by climbing over a high metal stile in the adjoining fence.

Turn left and make your way up the drive. When you come to the wide gateway just in front of the lawn at the hall, go through it and, turning half to the left, follow the faint line of a track across the grass, heading for the left side of the buildings, where you meet an earth road. You should now follow this good straight track for some considerable distance. Eventually, after nearly a mile, you reach the almost deserted buildings of Kiln Farm. The track crosses the yard and then bears quickly left, then right on leaving it. As you enter the next field you must turn left and follow a ditch along the left boundary of the field past well spaced oak trees. Keep straight on towards the large wood ahead of you and follow the outside edge of the wood, turning sharply to the right and then more gradually to the left as you start to go steadily downhill; all the time you keep the cultivated fields on your right.

When you come to a wide opening in the hedge beyond the end of the wood, turn through this to cross the stream running beside the hedge and then go on downhill following the stream on your right by way of a narrow but well used grass path. The stream now flows in a deep dell and you leave the field through an opening about 5 yards wide. Continue in the same way down the lower edge of the next field until you come to a point where the stream makes a ninety-degree turn to the right. Follow the same course yourself and walk beside the wire fence of a small grazing field. Turn left and continue along its longer side until you reach the main road through Stanstead village, beside the White Hart.

Turn right and walk along the street, passing the turning to Shimpling, until you come to a road junction where you need to be careful as you cross the road and turn left over Scotchford Bridge towards Glemsford. A little further on you cross another bridge and then start to climb the hill. The road bends sharply to the right past Place Farm and then even more sharply to the left towards the church in its commanding hill-top position.

Here you have to turn off to the right, just past the bend sign, along an earth track with a hedge on the right. After you pass the entrance to the small sewage works, the track becomes a narrow earth path lined with tall hedges on both sides. Beyond the end of the hedges you come out into a patch of damp ground with reeds and rough grasses, where the path winds ahead and keeps to the left of the small trees which form the boundary of the field on your left. You cross a small sleeper footbridge and then, as you come to a wider stream, have to turn left for about 20 yards to find another footbridge consisting of a rather narrow steel girder.

When you have crossed this you come to a grassy lane; turn left and walk up it between the hedge and stream on the left and a high bank on the right. As the track reaches some old iron railings it turns left over a bridge and you follow it uphill towards Hill Farm. Go through a gateway towards an impressive old barn and then turn right to reach the nearby road. Turn left and walk along this road to the centre of the large village of Glemsford, which is at a triangular green where three roads join.

From the southern edge of the green you continue in the same direction by taking a tarmac path which starts to the right of a pair of red-brick semidetached houses. Pass between the gardens of bungalows and modern houses and then cross a road and continue along an earth path, with a hedge and ditch soon joining it on the right, beside new building developments. Keep straight ahead following overhead cables as you come to a short length of residential road. Follow this and then, crossing the road, continue in the same line between some houses, where you turn left along a track behind their rear gardens.

You now come to open fields again and cross another footpath at a right angle to your route as you keep straight on to walk along the right side of a field on a narrow grass path, which takes you directly to a road.

On reaching the road, turn right and walk down it until you have gone about 100 yards past Court Farm. Now you turn left off the road to follow a lane flanked by banks and scattered trees on both sides. You pass a wood on the left and, as the lane bears slightly to the left and starts to dip towards the valley, the tower of Long Melford church shows clearly some distance ahead.

As you approach the valley bottom and pass a three-directional footpath signpost, you should keep straight ahead, leaving the lane, which bends to the right, and make your way through a small patch of woodland to a long narrow footbridge over the river Glem. A few yards beyond the bridge you have a stile to surmount and passing between small fields and pig pens you reach a road by means of a metal gate.

Turn left along the road between the buildings of Parsonage Farm until you pass the last barn on the right, and turn off the road to walk along the side of this, and follow the lower edge of the field, bearing first to the right and then sharply left to go uphill. When you reach a point where the shallow ditch by the hedge ends you have to go through a gap into the adjacent field and continue upwards, with the hedge now on your left. You have to turn left for a short distance and then right again to follow the boundary of the field until you arrive at a road as it passes some cottages.

Turn right and follow this road and after a few minutes walk you come to its junction with the main road from Long Melford to Clare. Cross the road and go straight ahead downhill, following an earth track on the sheltered eastern side of a high hedge.

After walking straight down the steady slope for nearly half a mile you reach a junction with another track by some old farm buildings and turn left to walk towards Long Melford. Through the hedges of this lane you soon have glimpses of Melford Hall as you approach the village. Reaching the main street at the lower end of the green, you have only to turn left and walk up beside the grass to be back where you began your walk.

John Andrews

7. Stowmarket

Distance: about 8 miles.
Ordnance Survey maps: 1:50,000 sheet 155; 1:25,000 sheets TM05 and TM06.
Grid reference: 044587.

This walk starts and finishes at the Recreation Ground in Stowmarket. The walk takes you to the hamlet of Dagworth, then skirts Old Newton and Stowupland and crosses the river Gipping and its tributaries several times. The Recreation Ground is beside the Finborough Road out of Stowmarket. There is a lay-by near some toilets.

Start walking across the recreation ground in a north-westerly direction along the second path from the right of the swings. Follow this path and at the other side of the recreation ground cross Recreation Road to join a footpath on the right of four bungalows. This footpath runs between houses and garages and comes out at Windermere Road. Here cross the road and walk up St Mary's Road opposite, continuing in the same direction. You will soon reach Gainsborough Road. You have now reached the end of the built-up area and from here the walk is all rural until you near Stowmarket at the end of the walk.

After crossing Gainsborough Road and heading slightly to the left, continue in the same general direction across a field and then beside a hedge and then a ditch and soon you will be walking beside the playing fields of Stowmarket High School. At the end of the playing fields turn right and continue until you reach a white cottage with a thatched roof. Here turn right along a concrete track to the front of the cottage. You will soon join a tarmac lane and continue along this until you reach the main A45 trunk road. Cross this carefully and at Nareys Nurseries turn to the left for a few yards, then right down Spikes Lane.

Continue down Spikes Lane, past a farm, and eventually across a stream. When you reach the railway line turn left and follow the lane right up to an attractive cottage. You appear to be walking right through the garden but walk to the right of the cottage and you will soon be in a meadow. Walk across this in the same direction, keeping the railway line on your right. Bear very slightly to the right and cross into the next meadow along a farm track, still keeping to the left of the line. Cross the next meadow, about halfway across keeping the hedge to your right. Continue to the gate at the end and you will rejoin a farm track. Follow this right round towards a farmyard. Here you will cross a brick-built bridge over a pretty stream. There are often cows in the enclosure opposite.

Turn to your right and proceed along a tarmac lane, under the railway line and then up the hill. If you pause at the top and

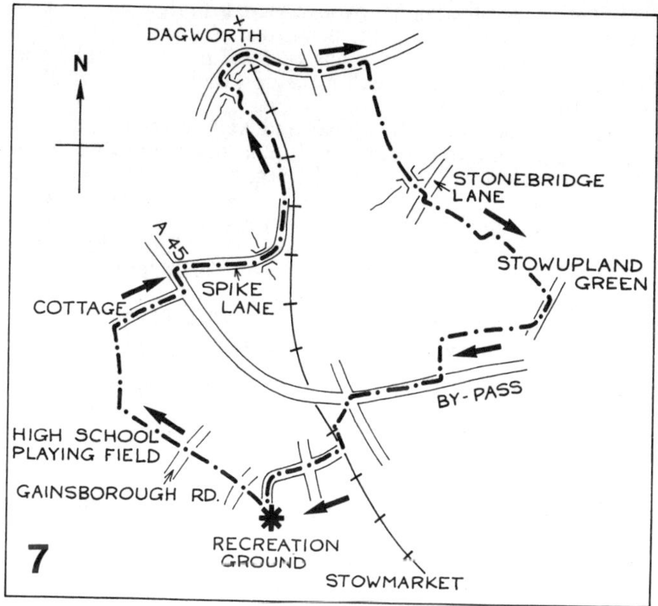

glance behind you, you will see a lovely view of the meadowland around Dagworth. When you reach the road at the end of the lane, cross this and take the road signposted to Mendlesham. After a few hundred yards turn to your right along a signposted path beside a field. About halfway down this at the signpost cross to the other side of the ditch, still continuing in the same direction. At the bottom you will find yourself in a lush meadow and straight ahead of you is a wooden bridge over the river Gipping. Cross the bridge and then a stile and another smaller bridge. At the road turn right for a yard or two and then left up a cart track beside a large fallen tree trunk.

Follow this cart track for about half a mile and at the top you will see a stile slightly to the left. Cross this and proceed straight ahead, through what is usually a muddy patch, to a gateway ahead of you. Go through this and just before the white farmhouse turn left and you will find yourself on Stowupland Green.

Turn to the right across the green and at the end walk a little way along Thorney Green Road. Immediately past the four bungalows on your right, fork to the right along a well worn footpath. At the junction of three fields fork left and head for the fence beside the Stowmarket bypass. Here turn right and walk at the top of the bank beside the main road. After a few hundred yards go through a novel swinging gate and proceed in the same direction but now along a well made-up farm track downhill to the road at the bottom.

Here turn left under the bypass and walk in the direction of Stowmarket until you reach the 30 mph restriction sign. Turn right and then fork right up a track to the railway line, then along a path beside the line until you reach the level crossing gates. Cross the line and proceed up this road (Crown Street) to the main road. Cross this and continue up Fairfield Hill to the road at the top. Here turn right and almost immediately turn left along Walnut Tree Walk. At the end of the houses on your left, turn left down a path beside the school and at the bottom of this you will find yourself back at the Recreation Ground.

Christine Eastall

8. Needham Market

Distance: about 8 miles.
Ordnance Survey maps: 1:50,000 sheet 155; 1:25,000 sheets TM05 and TM15.
Grid reference: 091549.

This walk starts and finishes at Needham Market station, where there is plenty of parking space. It is a very pleasant walk taking in part of the Gipping valley path along the river Gipping. It also goes through Priestley Woods, which are very old and in springtime are carpeted with bluebells. Some other rare wild flowers can also be found there.

Start by going through the tunnel to the left of the station, taking you under the railway line. When through the tunnel turn right and walk a few yards up to and past the hedge just ahead. Turn left here on to a well marked path and follow this to the riverside. Turn right, keeping along the riverbank, and walk between the river and the lake which is on your right.

When you reach the road turn left over the bridge and walk along the road, past Bosmere Mill, up to the Bailey bridge; turn right just before the bridge. (There is a footpath sign here.) This is now the canal, which joins the river again further up. Keep along the canal bank with the lakes on your right. You can soon see Bosmere Hall on the left across the canal. Still keeping to the canal path, go under pylon wires and over two bridges. Here the river joins the canal again. Keep to the riverbank up to Pips Ford. (Here a bridge crosses the river to a four hundred year old timbered cottage.) Keep this side of the river and turn right away

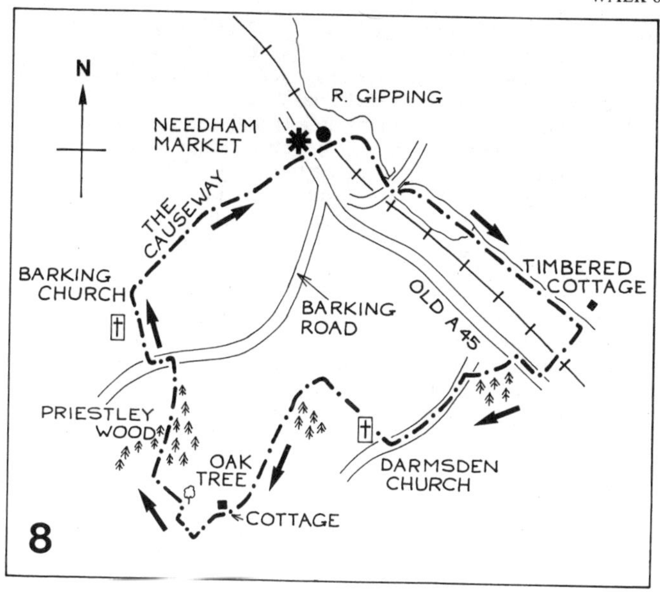

from the river, across a field along a very well marked track, up to the railway. Cross the railway track very carefully, then walk up to the road, which is the old A45. Turn right along the road for approximately 200 yards.

When you reach a large oak tree with a tin hut beside it on the left side of the road, cross the road and take the path uphill with a small conifer wood on your left. When you pause for breath at the top of the slope take time to glance at the view behind you.

Now follow the path into the wood and at a quiet country road turn left. This is a no through road going to Darmsden only. Keeping in the same direction, walk along the road for approximately three quarters of a mile to Darmsden church on the right. Turn right here, taking the path past the church and then up the hill. At the top near two small brick walls turn left and walk past a small conifer wood on your left. Keep straight on this path for approximately one mile. This wide path eventually narrows to a small grassy path with a cottage on your right. When past the cottage, cross the track that leads back to the road and go along the edge of a field opposite with the hedge on your left. It is not a very clear path just here but carry on by the hedge until you reach some cultivated blackberry bushes. Here turn right on the path in front of these blackberries. At the end keep going across the next field with the hedge on your right, then turn into a green lane (just before the footbridge). Go along the green lane and when you come into a field turn right along the edge for about 200 yards until you come to a small oak tree on your right.

Turn left here, taking a path in a straight line across the field. When you come to a junction of paths take the path on your right, which is on the left side of the hedge. This leads straight into Priestley Woods. These woods are particularly lovely in springtime when they are full of bluebells. Follow the path through the woods, turning right and then left and coming out on to a field. Turn right and keep along the edge of the field, which takes you down to Barking Road.

Cross the road and, turning left, walk along the road for a few yards, then take the next road on your right leading to Barking church. Go past the church, taking the right fork pathway at the top. You now enter The Causeway, which is a lovely path with trees either side. Carry on along this path for approximately one mile. When you come to a left turn in the path keep straight on over the footbridge. Carry straight on down this wide track towards Needham Market. You will pass an adventure playground on your left. Keep straight on past the Swan public house and out on to the High Street. Cross the road and the station is now straight ahead.

Helen Rowell

9. Kersey

Distance: 7½ miles.
Ordnance Survey maps: 1:50,000 sheet 155; 1:25,000 sheets TL94 and TM04.
Grid reference: 000441.

The walk starts and finishes at Kersey Splash. Kersey, charmingly set in the countryside of south Suffolk, is one of the county's prettiest villages. Try to make time for a visit to the pottery beside the Splash and to look around at the attractive cottages. There are two pubs in the village and bar food is available.

The walk takes you uphill to the church. Its south porch provides a fine example of flushwork and the wrought ironwork at the top of the steps frames a famous view of the village.

Where the church lane joins the road turn right, then left down Vale Lane. When the houses end, keep right down the lane into Kersey Vale. Follow the lane past some buildings to an iron gate beside a house. Just before this you will have seen a footpath sign pointing left across a bridge, but your path takes you straight

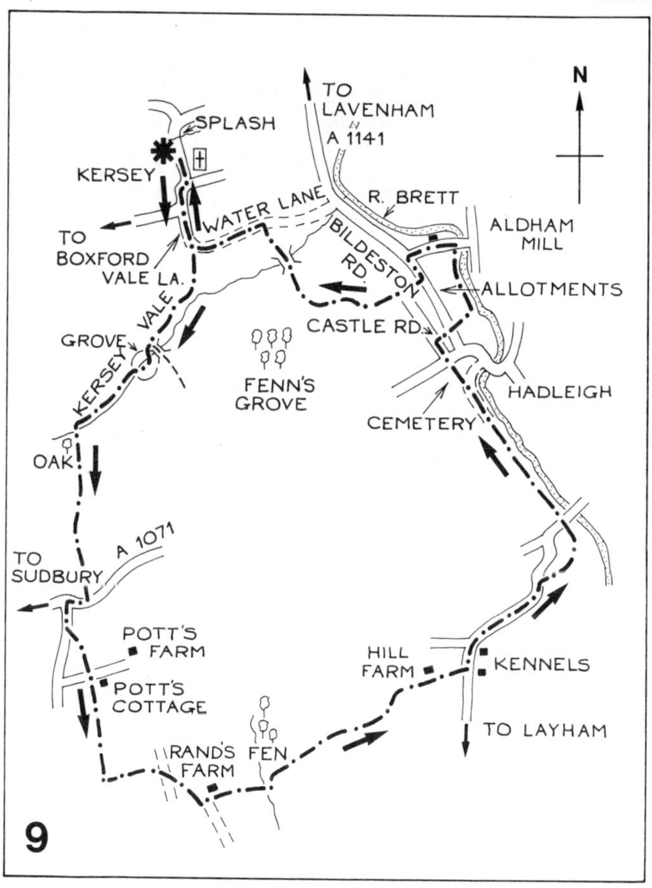

along through the gate with a hedge on your left, and where the hedge becomes a copse bear left into the trees. Cross a small stream by the sleeper provided and turn right. This route agreed with the farmer keeps you to the left of a copse used for rearing pheasants, so keep your dog on a lead.

When you leave the copse follow the edge of the field with Kersey Brook on your left. Pass one hedge and at the next one a mature oak on the far side of the brook marks where you cross over and with a hedge on your left make for the Hadleigh road.

At the road turn right and in a few yards take the road signposted to Polstead. In 300 or so yards the path runs through the garden of the house Buena Vista (the garden was made round the path!) past a wooden shed and follows the left-hand boundary of the field to a country lane close to Potts Cottages. Cross the lane and continue in the same direction. You have on your left a very deep drainage channel. At the end of the field (where the channel turns left) the path crosses the field in front. It is not visible on the ground for crops always obstruct but take your line from an oak tree which is nearly in line with the path you have been following. The line is about 10 yards to the left of the oak tree, where the ditch is bridged, giving you access into the next field, where you turn left and follow the headland track to the new tarmac road leading to gravel pits. Cross this and take the headland path, marked with a footpath sign, to Rands Farm. The path goes down the farm drive, then to the right of the black wooden garage and then into the green lane leading down into Bullocky Fen – a most attractive swampy area where you smell wild mint and are surrounded by tall horsetail ferns. The path is usually visible on the ground and it should be possible to avoid getting wet feet. Bear slightly left to the stream. Once you have stepped over, go right and leave the fen at a young oak tree. Turn left, then, following the field boundary, right. At the top of the steep little hill the path continues on the same line (the first 20 yards often obstructed with crops) along an obvious headland track with a hedge on the left.

When you arrive at a pond surrounded by trees on the right, the path continues with the field boundary on the right. Follow the headland path when it swings left and in 200 yards turn right into the next field and follow a narrow path clearly visible on the ground. The hedge on your left becomes the boundary of Hill Farm buildings. You arrive on the farm track, which takes you to a country lane at the kennels of the Essex and Suffolk Hunt.

Turn left on the lane and right as it drops downhill with good views of Hadleigh. Bear left at the foot of the hill and in 100 yards a footpath sign takes you along a field edge, through a pasture and beside a football field to the river Brett. A seat by a mill pool is a good picnic spot (and there is a pub about 300 yards away).

The route continues upstream past Toppesfield Bridge and along the riverbank through a wooded area — on a sunny summer day this is a very beautiful spot. When the path leaves the river you come on to a lane. Leave this through a children's play area and on to the edge of Hadleigh cricket field. Cross the Sudbury road and go up Castle Road, turning right down the first turning, Nursery Lane, across the Bildeston road and into the allotment area.

Turn left when you reach a jumble of smallholding sheds and

keep the boundary of the smallholding on your right until you reach the bank of the Brett again. Follow the Brett upstream to the ford at Aldham Mill.

Turn left away from the river and follow the farm road past Peyton Hall farm to the Bildeston road at a dangerous corner. Here you can go right along the road for several hundred yards, when a footpath sign will guide you to Water Lane; or turn left to where a footpath sign marks the entry (right) into a green lane.

Where the green lane finishes, the right of way goes across the diagonal of the small field and continues for 50 yards or so with a hedge on the right. At this point the line of the footpath is slightly to the right of Kersey church. You are making for a bridge across the stream in Kersey Vale but the slope of the land makes the bridge invisible. Kersey church will point the way and by 1984, when a bypass will run between you and the bridge, clear footpath signs should show the way.

Once over the bridge, go straight across a field to Water Lane, turn left to join Vale Lane and so back to Kersey Splash.

Alec O'Reilly

10. Stratford St Mary

Distance: 7 or 8 miles.
Ordnance Survey maps: 1:50,000 sheet 169; 1:25,000 sheet TM03.
Grid reference: 053353.

This walk starts on the A12 at Stratford St Mary. Cars may be parked in a suitable lay-by just past the Nayland turning or at the bottom of Stratford Hill. Many of the paths are signposted and the walking is easy except in very wet weather. It is on the Ipswich to Colchester bus route.

Start from the A12 north of Stratford St Mary, where a footpath sign indicates the path along the driveway to Stratford Hills Farm. Follow this track through the farm, then turn right, following a track northwards then eastwards to a wood. Follow the track skirting south of the wood and then keep straight ahead. There are good views on the left. Enter a lane on the right, through a gate. At the end of the lane another gate leads into a small meadow; cross the meadow to another gate (please close the gates) and then follow the track past Wheatland Farm to a road. Walk westwards along this rather busy road for a third of a mile. Now take the road northwards towards Holton St Mary for a short distance, and then turn left into a quiet bridleway going westwards for nearly a mile. Sometimes you may see some activity as the local races are held hereabouts. At the road turn left and walk down to Higham village. The pub is unfortunately closed

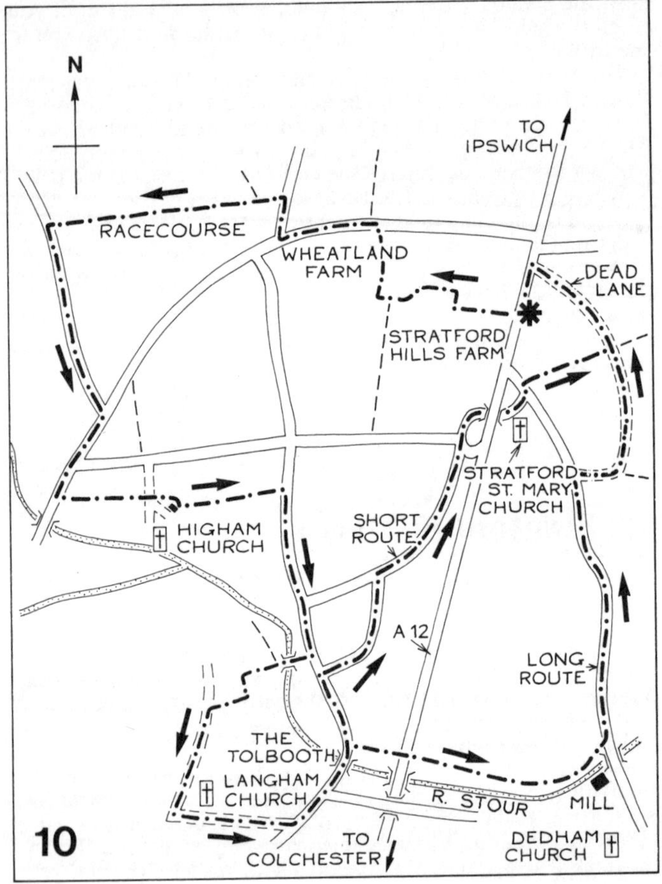

but there are many pretty cottages and a green. Go through the village and almost down to the bridge over the river Brett. Just before the bridge on the left a footpath sign directs the walker into a little hidden pathway which soon leads into a meadow by the river. Keep ahead to Higham church.

The path carries on over a wooden railing by the private house entrance. Cross the meadow to a stile and a track by the farm buildings. Walk eastwards beside the field to Stratford St Mary.

The river Brett has now joined the Stour in the water meadows below us. When the road is reached turn right, joining the main road by the pumping station, and continue past the Swan to the ruined mill where the Stour is crossed by the sluice and a concrete bridge. Keep straight ahead across the field, turn left up a wide track and then right by a hedge and finally into a sandy track which will lead up to Langham church. This was an area much favoured by Constable, the painter. After leaving the church follow the avenue eastwards to the Golden Gates on Gun Hill and go down the hill across the river bridge by the Talbooth.

Return through the village to the church and midway between the road junction past the church and the A12 a footpath sign indicates a path eastwards; after the first field is crossed a track leads upwards and joins Dead Lane coming up from the valley at Dedham. Follow this lane in a northerly direction through the woods and out on to the A12 near where the walk started.

A longer walk can be enjoyed by going under the underpass of the A12 near the Talbooth and walking beside the river to Dedham Mill. Here turn left towards Stratford St Mary and once round a bend turn right into a lane; after 300 yards the lane turns northwards — this is Dead Lane and by following it the A12 will be reached.

John Gibbs

11. Chelmondiston

Distance: 8 or 9 miles.
Ordnance Survey maps: 1:50,000 sheet 169; 1:25,000 sheet TM23.
Grid reference: 215370.

This walk starts from the Ipswich-Shotley road half a mile past Chelmondiston, where there is a suitable lay-by for car parking. It goes along the banks of the Orwell and Stour and over pleasant farmland tracks with extensive views of the shipping in Harwich harbour. It is on the Ipswich to Shotley bus route and there is ample opportunity for refreshments at several good pubs.

A few yards from the lay-by at a Civic Amenities Site a green lane leaves the road on the left. Follow this lane and go down past the buildings of Mill Farm. Then take a stile on the left, cross a small meadow to the stile opposite and cross a lane climbing the bank opposite to a road. Turn left and follow the road past Red House Farm (a wide expanse of the river Orwell is on the left) and continue for some distance. At Charity Farm take a tarmac road by the farm buildings and then follow this road, turning left (at a notice 'Shotley Hall footpath only') and past the farm buildings to a road.

Turn left along the road and almost immediately right into a

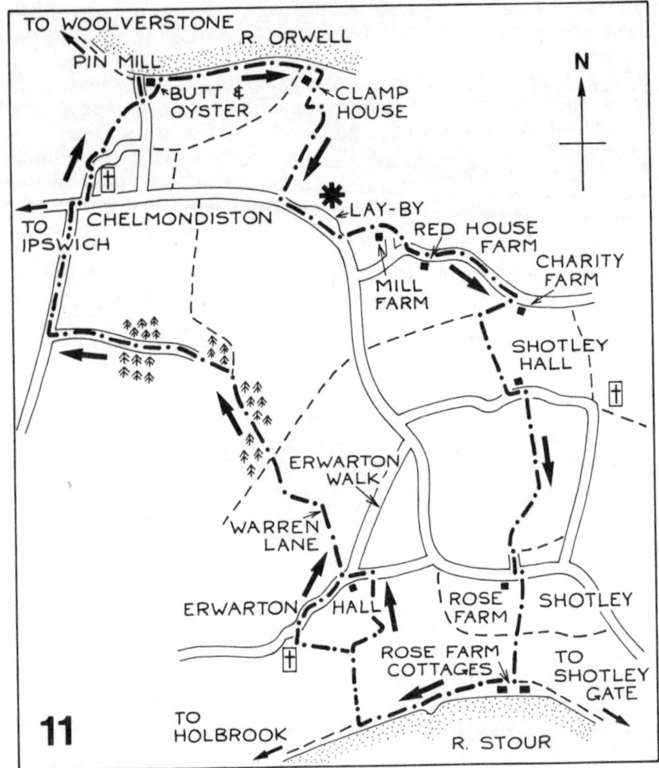

green lane. When the lane ends continue straight ahead on the headland of the field. Then the path descends to the other side of the hedge and continues until it crosses diagonally over the bottom section of the field (it is generally well defined by use). Cross the stream by a wooden bridge and follow the path uphill and go between the houses and bungalows. Turn left for a few yards (Garden Close) and then right (Orwell View Road) to get to the main road. (The Rose inn is on the right a few yards up the road.) Now turn left and enter a gravel road on the right through a farmyard (with a house on the left and farm buildings on the right) and continue down to the river wall (a private road used as a footpath). There are extensive views of Harwich and Parkeston Quay and several laid-up lightships.

At Rose Farm Cottages take the river wall on the right for some distance until nearly opposite Erwarton church. At a sluice, climb the stile and take the track inland. Either continue straight up to Erwarton Hall, skirting round a small reservoir and climbing a stile by an avenue of ancient chestnut trees and so reach the road, or, if preferred, cross the footbridge and cross two fields to a lane leading up to Erwarton church (Anne Boleyn's heart was reputedly buried here). Then follow the road to the right to Erwarton Hall, with its unusual gatehouse. (Watch the traffic on this winding road.)

Straight in front of the hall is Erwarton Walk, but take Warren Lane, a farm track left (or west) of the gatehouse. Follow this track for some distance past a cottage, a plantation on the left and then a small wood on the right and across a field to a white cottage. Then follow the track on the left through a wood and to a T junction. Take the road on the right to Chelmondiston. Go across the main road to the church or visit the village inns or shops. There is a path and a road down to the famous Butt and Oyster inn at Pin Mill.

From this inn return up the road a short distance to where a guard rail marks some steps up to the cliff top. Behind a bungalow, follow the path to the left and then for a long distance along the cliff top and finally descend to Clamp House. Follow the river wall in front of the lawn and over a sluice, then turn inland around a field edge. Cross a field to the Alder Carr, continuing inland beside it and through a fir plantation, and then a track will lead on to the road near the start of the walk.

John Gibbs

12. Stanton

Distance: nearly 12 miles.
Ordnance Survey maps: 1:50,000 sheet 144; 1:25,000 sheets TL97 and TM07.
Grid reference: 967735.

The ramble described here consists of a circuit around the fields and four villages of north Suffolk, starting from the recently much enlarged village of Stanton.

To find the starting point, turn off the main road from Bury St Edmunds to Diss, the A143, into the centre of the village and look for the war memorial in the triangular space at the crossroads. There is no difficulty in finding a place to park near here, before you walk southwards down the Street, passing a turning to the right and keeping straight on to reach the end. Here the Street becomes Wyken Road and bends gently to the right; you should leave it by forking to the left along a gravel track. At the end of this short track, keep straight ahead past a long low bungalow on your left, to enter a slightly overgrown depression which very quickly becomes a sunken lane with banks which soon rise to a remarkable height on both sides. This curiosity is known as the Grundle and has apparently been a public highway for very many years, although it seems to have originated as a natural watercourse. The surface of the path is at first sandy and then as you continue it may be muddy in places and increasingly gives you the feeling that you are walking along a dried-up river bed. Pass under a brick bridge and continue ahead through an opening where a tractor track descends to cross the path, and then on into a more shaded stretch. You will quite soon see what looks like a better used and wider path turning away to the right but you must still go straight on although the path is now narrower and you start to climb gently up a sloping ravine, eventually to leave it by coming up into a field on your left.

You are nearly at the end of this field and have to turn left along its boundary with a hedge on the right along a grass path which soon becomes wider and then begins to bend right as you pass the ruins of former farm buildings. You are now in what was once called Wash Lane, but not for very long. When you reach the end of the field on the right, about 150 yards past the ruins, a wide opening over the ditch on your right enables you to turn right into the next field. Sadly the lane that once ran south-eastwards from here was ploughed up many years ago and you will probably have to use the much narrower strip of grass which runs beside the ditch, following its route for nearly half a mile. You will come to a stretch of the lane which has survived, though it is much neglected and in need of clearance and you may have to step over the ditch to the right and walk along the side. When the lane becomes a well used farm road, near a strange high hump which is a remnant of the wartime airfield close by, continue to its end and turn right to reach a concrete road near Potash Farm.

Turn left along this and then left again at the road junction. Soon the road you have joined bends to the left and you will see here a wooden signpost indicating a footpath to the right leading from a stile along the broken surface of an old airfield road. The bleakness of this path should soon be lessened by the young trees planted beside it. When you reach the right-hand end of a belt of trees you will be helped by a signpost to discover a narrow earth path which leads to the left down the centre of the trees. Closer inspection will show you that it is in reality an overgrown track. On emerging from the trees keep straight on for a further 30 yards until you see a path going off to the right beside a low wire mesh fence along the edge of a wood. From here to the road you are assisted in your direction finding by thoughtfully placed waymarks. Cross a track as you leave the wood and walk on

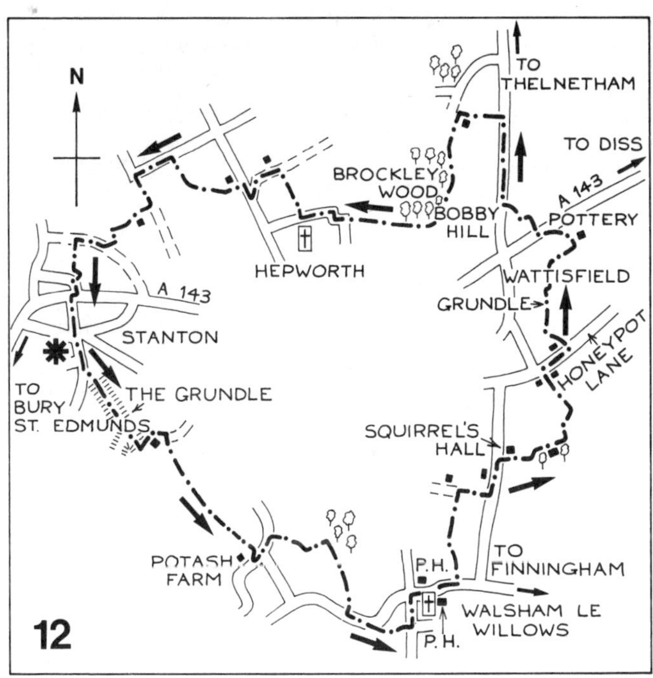

gently downwards on a grass path, which at first follows a high hedge and then a ditch between two large fields. At the far end of these cross another grass track and go along a winding path through a small wood past a delightful little pool until you are walking beside the fence of the field on your right. Not far beyond, you cross a wooden footbridge over a stream and then a stile brings you to the road, where you should turn left towards Walsham le Willows.

Approaching the village, the road bends sharply to the left, but you will probably prefer to use the footpath which leads straight on here from a stile constructed in a now immovable kissing gate. The path follows the left side of a grazing field at first by a small stream and then, as the stream bends to the left, goes on ahead over the field, passing electricity poles to your right, to reach another kissing gate by the road just south of the church. Turn towards the church, which looks all the more lovely because of the carefully tended graveyard, and if you are a lover of old buildings you are sure to find its light fresh interior and the exquisitely carved nave roof well worth inspection.

Walsham le Willows is one of those places that it is very hard to leave behind you. The road to Finningham that you take from the crossroads by the church contains a fascinating mixture of old buildings of varying ages as well as a couple of pubs. The road bends left and right by the Congregational chapel and you have to take a signposted path to the left beyond a row of painted railings just before a whitewashed cottage. This track at first leads past garages and gardens and then becomes less 'civilised' as it comes to open fields, bends sharply left and right and leads on unflanked by hedge or ditch. When you come to a T junction near the derelict Fishpond Barn turn right along a shady track and walk towards the road to Wattisfield.

Turn left at the road and stay on it as far as the farm at Squirrel's Hall, passing a bungalow on the left just before you reach it, and turn into the lane on the right, which leads to and beyond the house, sheds and paddocks of the farm. The lane winds onwards between fields, with lengths of hedge punctuated by gaps on either side. If you look hard at a copse of trees on your right you will see the derelict cottage at Burnt House and at the adjacent barn the lane comes to an end. Careful navigation will be needed for the next few minutes. Go straight on from the barn along the right edge of the field by a ditch and pass under overhead cables close to a pylon. At the end of the field turn left and walk alongside the boundary for about 70 yards to a point where a wide opening over the ditch on your right allows you to enter the next field. From here the line of the ploughed-up lane goes diagonally half-left to the left end of the hedge on the other side. As you reach this apparent end of the hedge you will see that it is actually a right-angle bend and you should turn right as you round the corner and follow the hedge until you come to the end of the remaining lane and turn left along its well grassed surface in the direction of Wattisfield. You can now walk straight ahead for about a third of a mile along a track which becomes rather muddy and better shaded before you come to some cottages near a road junction.

Turn right and walk up the road called Honeypot Lane for nearly a quarter of a mile. Just past some cottages on the left a green metal sign by a gateway into a field on the left tells you that this is a footpath to the village. It is a narrow grass path leading down the left side of the field and continuing in the same way beside the next narrower one before you reach a footbridge over Wattisfield Grundle. This is less spectacular than the Stanton version and has a stream along it for much of the year, so you have to walk beside it rather than along it. Turn right at the end of the bridge and you will find a narrow grass path following the lower edge of the fields towards the village. When you come nearly level with the church, whose tower can be seen above the trees to the left, your path turns right and then bends to the left to continue beside the rather insignificant ditch that is here the only trace of the Grundle. When you come to a metalled path, turn right up an earth track, where a signpost directs you towards the pottery. Wattisfield had a pottery in Roman times; the remains of a Roman kiln can be seen on the grass as you turn to the left on reaching the buildings and the present business continues that tradition. Indeed it seems possible that pottery making was practised here by the Beaker people some four thousand years ago.

From the pottery walk down the road to the A143 and turn left towards the crossroads. When you reach a T junction sign on the right you will see a ditch leading away from the road and up the hill between open fields. You might prefer to walk on to the crossroads and have a look at more of the village and seek refreshment and then turn right at the crossroads to rejoin the route just beyond Bobby Hill. If not, you should turn right at the T junction sign and then almost immediately cross the ditch and continue up the slope with the ditch on your right, turning left then right with it to reach the top. Here you need to turn left for about ten paces and then right again through a narrow gap in the hedge before going on along the left side of the next field to the Thelnetham road. When you have turned right you will accompany this road for exactly half a mile.

About 200 yards past a whitewashed cottage on the left you will come to a metalled road leading left towards a farm. Follow this road and, when you reach the farm buildings, turn left and walk along a poorly surfaced road towards Brockley Wood. When you come to the trees keep on the outside of the wood along a pleasant grass track. The track soon moves away from the wood to stay beside the ditch on your left but then makes its way back towards it, now becoming narrower and less clearly marked. As you reach the trees again you start to bend round to the right, following the outside edge of the wood once more along a narrow strip of grass. By the time you reach the end of the wood and cross a grassy lane you are facing due west and will now have to make quite a long crossing of an extremely large field. If you can make out the tower of Hepworth church with its squat pyramid-shaped spire amongst the trees ahead of you, you should aim exactly for that. On reaching the road continue along it past Grange Farm to the church.

Opposite the church gate you leave the road again by turning right and making your way along a grass track until you come to another similar track at a T junction, where you turn left and walk past a red-brick house. The track becomes an earth road now and, bending to the left, arrives at the northern end of the village street. Turn right towards a telephone kiosk and only about 50 yards past this you must climb a metal gate into a field on the left, follow the right edge of the field straight ahead and then go on across to the left-hand end of the hedge in front of you. When you have negotiated this you should turn half-right and head for the far right corner of the grazing field you have now entered. About 30 yards before the end of the hedge along the right-hand side a gateway leads into the recreation field. You must continue on almost the same diagonal line across this field, keeping to the left of the oak tree, towards a narrow gap in the hedge in the further left corner. When you have stepped through the opening you must go straight along the edge of the new field beside a ditch until you reach the road by way of a sleeper over the ditch beside it.

Walk along the road to the left until you can turn left again along another open grassed track where the road turns sharply in the opposite direction. At the end of the long field on the right you should turn right up a track beside the hedge towards an electricity pylon near the ruined barn at New Hall. Go straight into the field behind the barn and cross it diagonally to reach a low fence in the far left corner. The path beyond the fence has been ploughed up and you have only the rough grass beside a ditch to use as you follow the ditch straight ahead and then to the left towards a wooden footbridge. When you have crossed the bridge, turn right to walk on the narrow strip of grass on the upper edge of the field. Soon the path meets a hedge and grows wider and then comes to an open earth road, where you turn right at the signpost. About 200 yards from here, opposite the first hedge that leads away at ninety degrees to the right, you must turn left to head down across the open field using a path whose only visible sign may be a crop boundary. Turn to the left at the bottom and follow the hedge round to a narrow metalled lane. You have only to walk on down this and cross the main road at a staggered junction to find yourself in a few minutes back in the centre of Stanton.

John Andrews

13. Woodbridge

Distance: about 6 miles.
Ordnance Survey maps: 1:50,000 sheet 169; 1:25,000 sheet TM24.
Grid reference: 273487

Woodbridge is one of the most attractive small towns of Suffolk. This walk takes you on paths out of the town centre, along the banks of the river Deben, circles across farmland and

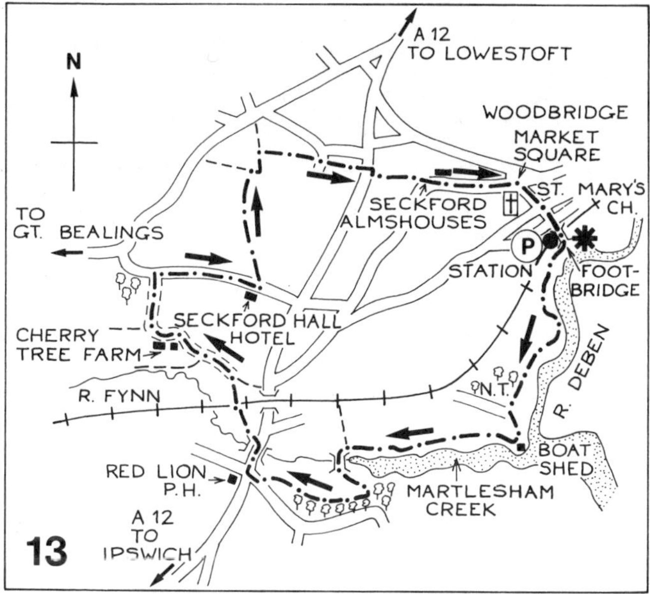

ends by going back through the town, with its beautiful old buildings.

The walk starts at Woodbridge railway station. There is ample free parking close to the station, at the Deben Swimming Pool, which is in Station Road.

At the railway station take the footbridge over the railway line and go down to the river and harbour. With the harbour on the left, take the tarmac path south along the river. The path soon leaves behind all the bustle and boats of the harbour and continues along meadows and river, with fine views of the river Deben and Woodbridge Tide Mill.

The path now enters a wooded area. The small area ahead and to the right is National Trust property. However, we take the path to the left and down to the water again and Kyson Point. This is private property, so keep to the public footpath. At the point where a wooden boathouse stands, take the path right and into Martlesham Creek. It can be rather wet here at high tide, but the path soon ascends to the river wall again. Follow this right along to the head of the creek and bear left over the sluice gates. Pause awhile here, for the view back down the creek is very rewarding. Watch for the bird life: herons, shelduck and oyster catchers are among those birds which find this a favourite spot.

Continue now towards Martlesham Wood, through the stile, and in a few yards turn right. Turn right again after about 150 yards, keeping near the right-hand edge of the wood. At the end of the wood is another stile and the pathway enters a nursery field. Cross the field, keeping the hedge on the right, to the iron gate (remembering to close it after use). Turn right on to the road and walk towards the traffic lights and the Red Lion public house.

Turn right on to the main A12 road and in a short distance cross the road at the river bridge. Just past the telephone box, turn left between two cottages. This small lane ends in a footpath left of a garage. Cross the narrow stream and head for the white-painted stile at the foot of the railway embankment. Carefully cross the line and enter the field. The path is now diagonally left, aiming for the second telegraph pole from the far corner of the field on the right. Cross to the farm track by a hedge and turn left towards a farm.

At Cherry Tree farm follow the track around to the right, passing a new bungalow on the right, and going on up the track. This will lead to a metalled road with a footpath sign at the entrance.

Turn right on to the road. Unfortunately there is no footpath here, but the road is usually very quiet. After half a mile along this road, Seckford Hall Hotel will be seen on the right. It has a beautiful Tudor facade and was built about 1530 by Thomas Seckford's father.

Opposite the hotel, take the second farm track on the left, leading to a farm and its buildings. The footpath is on the right of the houses and leads straight across the field to the far hedge. Turn right at the hedge and within about 30 yards turn left over a stile — this is rather concealed in an overgrown hedge. Cross the field to the stile opposite, then go right again over a second stile. Keeping a hedge on the left, keep on the path at the edge of the field towards a white cottage.

At a track turn right and in a few yards turn left into a tree-lined path. This delightful path ends at the very busy A12 road. Cross straight over to the right-hand edge of a clump of trees and down to Bilney Road.

The rest of the walk now takes you through the built-up area of the town of Woodbridge. Turn right in Bilney Road, then left into Bullards Lane, left again into Naunton Lane and immediately right into Colletts Walk. At the end of this road a small tarmac path leads to Seckford Street. Continue straight ahead, passing the Seckford Almshouses up to your left. Enter the Market Square, with its many fine old buildings, with the Shire Hall and well in the centre. Turn right in the square, down the steps to St

Mary's church. Turn left and walk through the peaceful churchyard to the top of Church Street. The fine building of the Woodbridge Abbey School is on your right. Walk down the hill, cross over at the traffic lights, down Quay Street, and soon the station will be in sight — where the walk started.

Paddy Bills

14. Framlingham

Distance: full walk 12 miles, with shorter versions of 8 and 10 miles.
Ordnance Survey maps: 1:50,000 sheet 156; 1:25,000 sheets TM26 and TM36.
Grid reference: 286638.

This is a circular walk from Framlingham Castle to Parham. It is possible to shorten the walk by making short cuts which are described. There is a public house, the Willoughby Arms, in Parham, a short distance from the route, where refreshments can be obtained. The walk described is on public rights of way, but where there appear to be local variations to avoid crops these are mentioned as well.

The start is at the entrance road to Framlingham Castle. Walk up the drive. Just before the bridge leading to the castle door, take the turnstile on the left. Go down the hill and cross the dry moat by a footbridge, and follow the well used path across the castle grounds to a footbridge and stile in the perimeter hedge. Just beyond the stile several paths meet. Bear slightly to the left and, keeping the mature hedge, which is almost a wood, on your right, follow the well trodden path in a generally northerly direction. In 200 yards cross a footbridge with integral stiles and enter Framlingham College sports field. Turn left immediately and follow the boundary almost to the road. Go left through the hedge and continue along the path parallel to the road, through rough and marshy ground which surrounds The Mere, which can be seen on the left.

In about a quarter of a mile, after passing a small belt of willows the path turns right and joins the road. Cross the road and follow the track opposite, which shortly bears round to the right. In a few yards take a well walked path to the left through rough pasture to the road, just south of the entrance to Framlingham College. Turn left and follow the road. Continue on, passing the road on the right leading to 'Saxtead Mill 2 miles', but take the next road to the right. Go down the hill and in a quarter of a mile reach a T junction. There is a grass triangle here. Turn left but almost immediately follow the footpath sign leading half-right alongside a mature hedge. Very soon turn right at another sign, still following the same hedge on the right. Climb the hill to the road.

Turn right, pass the corner house and go round the bend in the road to pass an old cottage. In another 100 yards, by telephone pole number 3, go into the field on the left through a gap and immediately turn right to follow the hedge parallel to the road. Go through the next gap in a cross hedge and follow the hedge on the left to reach a broken-down stile in the shade of a large oak tree. Beyond the stile turn right and go between the hedge and the rabbit fence protecting a young plantation to the cart track in front of Hill Farm. At this point walk a few yards to the left and find the concrete hardstanding at the corner of a very large field.

The public path lies diagonally across the field to a pollarded oak tree close to an electricity pole. (If you are still in doubt, this is the oak tree which appears to the left of a prominent Scots pine.) If the direct route is obstructed by crops, follow the field boundary on the right, passing the farm buildings and skirting the wood. At the end of the field turn left alongside the hedge and go through the narrow gap and culvert at the foot of the oak tree. Go down the edge of the field, with the hedge on the right, to the garden of Lampardbrook Farm, which you skirt to the left, and turn left on to the farm drive and walk out to the road.

Turn left along the road and in 50 yards bear right along a well defined track to a house. Pass the house and follow the cart track to a clump of poplar trees. You have now reached the river Ore, which can be seen on your left. Follow the riverbank and in about 100 yards notice a concrete footbridge over the river, but continue straight on following the river in a wide sweep to the left. In another 300 yards turn right and leave the river. The path lies alongside an embankment of the former Framlingham branch railway line; there are many traces of the disused track in this valley. The old railway bridge over the river has been demolished and the embankment may be levelled before long. If such is the case, strike out at right angles to the river in a south-easterly direction, towards a cottage.

At the end of the embankment follow the cart track directly towards the cottage. Just before reaching it, bear slightly right and go through a gate to the road.

Continue along the road. In about 50 yards reach a T junction and turn left. On the left at this corner is Niggles House. This is an old railway cottage – note the LNER sign over the door. Follow the road, over the river Ore, round a bend to the left with a large lay-by on the right. Pass a pair of flinty cottages on the left and almost immediately turn right off the road up a somewhat overgrown bridleway at the edge of the woods. Follow the field boundary with the woods on the right, pausing to enjoy the views

behind you, and after passing a concrete farmyard on the right turn right on to a cart track and in 100 yards reach the road opposite Manor Farm. Go right along the road for about a quarter of a mile to where the road makes a broad sweep to the left. Here, on the left, is a wide verge where a cart track bears away slightly to the left of the road. There is a green footpath sign, reading 'Parham Woods'.

Take the track, but in about 50 yards, where the track turns left into a disused pit, keep straight on along a narrow headland, with a hedge of limes on the left. Go up to the end of the field and turn left through a narrow gap in the hedge on the left, and continue in the same direction as before but with, on the right, a hedge of mature trees. Very soon you will join a cart track, which, after a slight rise, passes on the right a pond and a farmhouse, which originally formed a wing of the seventeenth-century Parham House. Follow the track along the edge of the wood to the corner in about 100 yards.

At the corner of the wood the public right of way leads across the field in front of you to the cart track which can be clearly seen leading straight up the hill on the other side of the shallow valley. If the field is in crop it may be easier to divert from the public path and turn right along the cart track beside the wood, and at the junction of tracks, where the wood ends, turn left, pass an implement shed and go over a bridge across a narrow stream to reach the public path you have already observed. If you need to take the diversion, look behind you as you approach the implement shed — you will see the two pillars which once marked the entrance drive to Parham House.

Climb the hill, with Parham Wood a field away on the right. At a point opposite the end of Parham Wood a cart track joins on the right. This point is marked **A** on the sketch map.

If you want the shortest walk, continue straight on and, where the track turns to the left, go forward to the right side of the hedge in front of you and follow it to the end of the field. Cross a wooden sleeper bridge and continue straight across the next field to meet the road immediately to the right of the cottage which can be seen opposite. Turn left and in three quarters of a mile reach North Green, and thence to Framlingham by the route which is described later.

For the walk to Parham, take the cart track on the right, southward, alongside Parham Wood. At the southern corner of the wood there are a few derelict buildings. From there, if you look half-left, you will see Parham church with, on the hill a little to the right, Parham Moat Hall. You will pass these buildings later. Your path now lies almost due south across a wide field. Look across the field to the wood beyond. Make for the left-hand end of that wood — you may find a crop division which is approximately on the line of the path. Having crossed the field you will find yourself at the top of the former railway cutting. Look carefully to left and right and find timber steps cut into the bank. Go down to the floor of the cutting. There are also steps up on the other side (that footpath leads through the woods, across the Ore and out to the road). However, you turn left and keep in the cutting till it ends and then follow the field boundary to the corner of the field. Do not cross the ornamental fence in front of you, which leads into a narrow meadow, again the former railway, but go left for 10 yards to the left-hand side of the thick hedge which formed the northern boundary of the railway. Follow this thick hedge, which is on your right, along a narrow path through scrub which was once a green lane. It becomes in 300 yards Brick Lane, with houses on the right, and shortly after joins the road. Turn right and very soon reach a three-way road junction.

For those who seek refreshments, the Willoughby Arms is straight on, over the bridge to the T junction and 300 yards down the road to the left.

Take the road to the left (for those returning from the Willoughby Arms, it is the road to the right). On your right near the junction note Church Farm, parts of which are fifteenth-century, and the delightful pargeting by the windows. Turn right up the lane towards the church. Pause at the lychgate to see the village stocks housed there; they are hung in the roof. Do not enter the churchyard but continue through the kissing gate into a meadow. Keep straight on, with the hedge on the left, to a stile beside a gate and into the next field. Cross that field, keeping the narrow stream on your right, to another stile by a gate. In the next field skirt to the right of the grassy knoll, then climb the hill, bearing round to the left, passing close to an electricity pole, and reach a gate at the top of the field, with Moat Hall 100 yards beyond. At this point look back at the valley and view the church nestling in the village, with in the distance Parham Wood and the tumbledown buildings where you were half an hour ago.

Enter the pasture and pass Moat Hall on your right. This is an excellent example of a moated Tudor manor house. Wend your way round the moat to the right and cross the stile to the drive which leads to Moat Hall, where in niches on either side of the ancient gateway two wild men stand sentinel. Turn left along the drive and after passing the farm buildings turn left on to a farm road to reach the public road by a water tower.

Go straight on along the road, past a poplar grove, to Silverlace Green. At the triangle go right along the road signed 'Cransford and Bruisyard'. If you want to shorten the walk by about 2 miles,continue along this road for about a mile to North Green, where you will be able to take the bridleway to Framlingham, which is described later.

About 100 yards from the signpost at the road junction, and immediately before the woods, go right into the field and walk beside the wood to its end. The next part of the walk is across a former airfield and you are faced by a very large field with not many landmarks. Stand at the corner of the woods with your back to the direction from which you have come. A little to the right of straight ahead, and about 100 yards away, is a small clump of trees and bushes. Make for these trees; you will find that they surround a very small pond. The route of the public path is just to the right of the barn visible in front, but it is easier to go a little to the right to reach a short concrete hardstanding not far away. Follow the concrete towards the barn and reach the main concrete perimeter taxiway. Turn left and then follow this wide concrete road, passing the barn, and thence bending round to the right for about half a mile. On the right in the distance is a hangar and the former control tower, and on the left you will see a building which is currently used for private flying.

The public right of way leaves the concrete airstrip and crosses the field to the north, but most people continue along the runway to reach the road that intersects it. Turn left and go down the hill on the road to the T junction, where you turn left on to a road signed 'Cransford and Framlingham'.

Walk along the road for about half a mile to the point where the road makes a sharp right turn. Go straight on along a lane marked 'No through road'. Pass Stone House Farm and just beyond the farm follow the gravel farm track round to the left, which forms a lane with hedges on both sides (there are oaks on the right). The track is dead straight for a little under half a mile, until by a group of hawthorns on the right the track gives a slight kick to the left. At this point the right of way goes diagonally across the field on the right. However, it will probably be easier to continue along the track and follow the next hedgeline on the right. When you reach that next hedgeline it is best to check your position. The hedge contains a number of mature oak trees, and the farm track which continues turns left immediately beyond the hedge for about 20 yards and then goes half-right to sweep away to the south-west. Having reached this point, follow the hedge with the oak trees, keeping it on the left, and at the end of the field cross a ditch in front of you and enter a large field.

The line of the public footpath heads across the field towards the tallest tree in the woodland, which is half-left as you stand with your back to the ditch. Here, if the route is difficult because of crops, it is suggested that you turn left and follow the ditch which you have just crossed to the next hedge, where you turn right and follow the hedge on your left, following round a dog-leg in the hedge and on to cross a culvert and join a broad grassy track at the corner of the woods towards which you have been making. Follow the grassy track with the wood on your left until just before the first pink-washed farmhouse. Turn left to pass in front of the house on a cart track, then right, through the farmyard, and out to reach the road at North Green. Go left along the road for about 30 yards to the bridleway sign 'Framlingham'.

This is **North Green**, where the shorter alternatives rejoin the walk. Take the lane towards Home Farm, which is the bridleway to Framlingham. Pass the duck pond and the farm and at the end of the lane turn right along the cart track. There is a sign here. Follow the edge of the wood and then a field boundary. Turn left at a bridleway sign and follow the ditch on the left towards St John's Grove. At the end of the field go over a culvert and turn left for 50 yards to the Grove. Skirt the edge of the wood westwards and then a hedge on your left till just before the next cross hedge, where you turn left over the culvert and continue on the other side of the hedge. Keep alongside the hedge, right and left round a small dog-leg, and you will reach a grassy track where it makes a right-angle turn. To the left the track leads to New Barn, which can be clearly seen, but you go straight ahead. This pleasant grassy lane is called Coldhall Lane. In about three quarters of a mile reach the road, the B1119 (Framlingham to Saxmundham), on the outskirts of the town.

The quickest way back to the start is straight down the road to the castle. To avoid road walking however, turn right along the road for just over 100 yards and turn left at a cart track just beyond the houses: there is a footpath sign here. The right of way is down the cart track for 150 yards and then left across the field. To avoid the crops, walkers could turn left behind the houses and follow the field boundary to the corner, turn right along the hedge for about 50 yards and then left over a footbridge into the recreation ground. Follow the recreation ground boundary and thence a narrow footpath out to the road. Turn right along the road for 200 yards, and enter a large field on the left. Follow the hedge on the left, which towards the corner of the field swings round to the right. Go left over a stile and almost straight ahead is the stile leading over a bridge into the castle grounds. Cross the stile and retrace your steps to the starting point.

Geoff Pratt

15. Leiston

Distance: about 9½ miles.
Ordnance Survey maps: 1:50,000 sheet 156; 1:25,000 sheet TM46.
Grid reference: 447625.

Leiston is a small town with a population of about five thousand, with some heavy industry. In the nineteenth century it was famous for the steam traction engines built there. The ruins of Leiston Abbey date from 1388 and are in the care of the Department of the Environment. The attractive coastline has some sandy beaches and provides excellent walks to the north and south.

This walk starts at the large free car park on the north side of Sizewell Road, Leiston.

Leave the car park in a northerly direction along built-up side roads to cross the railway at a level crossing, and turn left into Westwood Road. 300 yards along on the right is a footpath signposted 'Hill Farm 1 mile'. Follow the path, passing nurseries on the left. Cross a track and pass between fields planted with soft fruit bushes, and then continue across fields to reach a metalled road at Aldhurst Farm. Turn right and in 100 yards turn left on to a track signposted 'Leiston Abbey'. Pass on your right first the ruined abbey, then a track and car park. The path then crosses a field, at the end of which is a hedge. Turn right along the north side of the hedge until you join a road (B1122 Leiston to Yoxford).

Turn right and in 200 yards turn left into a metalled lane signposted 'East Bridge'. Follow the lane for three quarters of a mile, until you reach a track on the right with hedges on both sides. Follow the track for 100 yards, passing on the left a small cottage called 'The Round House' (although the house is rectangular) and then bear right (to walk in a southerly direction). The track passes Upper Abbey Farm on the right and eventually joins a road at a bend, with the CEGB laboratories on the right. Continue in a southerly direction along the road for 500 yards until, at a road junction with cottages nearby, you must turn left into a lane (Sandy Lane). Follow the lane and, on reaching Rackham Lodge on the left, bear right and walk through a wooded area, at the end of which Sizewell power station will be seen forward on the left. Pass under overhead power cables and on joining another lane turn right and continue until a road is reached. Turn left (now walking in an easterly direction) and in 300 yards pass the Vulcan public house.

A short distance further on, at Sizewell village, the road turns left (north). Do not turn left but leave the road and keep straight on, bearing slightly right. The shore and the sea will be seen ahead. Turn right (south) and follow the grassy path for 350 yards, passing coastguard cottages on the right. In front of a largish house on the cliff, turn right up the cliff and then left to pass the house and then turn right into a track passing a caravan site on the right. In a short distance turn left at a junction with another track and walk beside a wall on the left. Sizewell Hall is in the ground beyond the wall.

When the track divides, bear right through heathland, cross a track and bear right at the next two divisions of the track to pass cottages on the left. Shortly after passing the cottages the track joins another from the left. Keep straight on until the path divides, bear right and in a short distance a bridge will come into view. The bridge carried a railway line, now removed. Pass under the bridge and turn right. The path now passes a golf course, at first on the left and later on the right. A line of trees on the right at right angles to the path is known as Forty Acre Belt. Pass this and then under overhead power cables. As the cables are passed a converging high hedge will be seen on the left. A path follows this hedge and where the two paths join make a U turn. Keeping the hedge on the right, follow it for a short distance and then turn

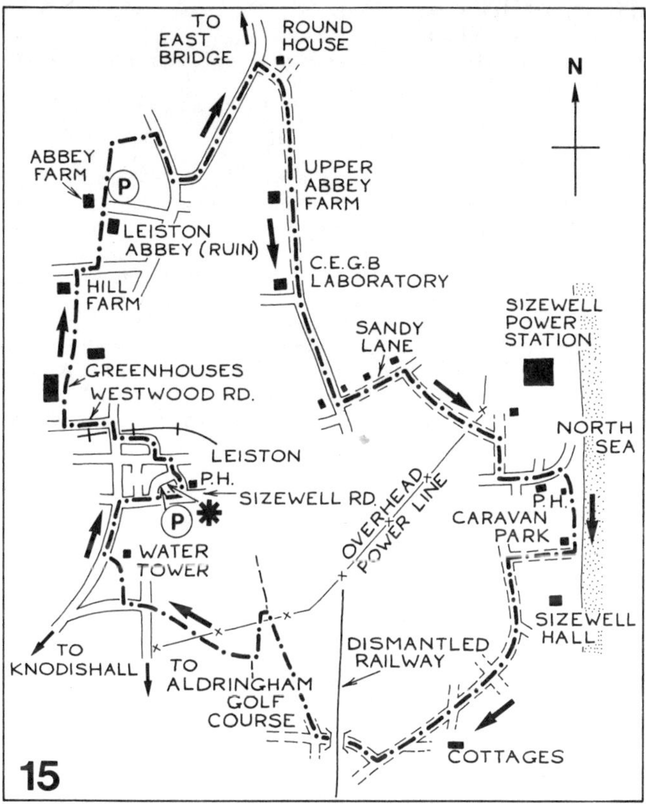

right through a gap to follow another hedge on your left-hand side. The path again passes under the overhead power line and eventually passes between some houses to join a road.

Cross the road and walk along Goldings Lane for about 200 yards, then turn right into a footpath with private gardens on either side. Pass a water tower on the right and continue between houses to join Haylings Road. Turn right until you reach Cross Street, turn right again and continue to Sizewell Road and return to the car park.

George Handley

16. Southwold

Distance: about 10 miles.
Ordnance Survey maps: 1:50,000 sheet 156; 1:25,000 sheets TM47 and TM57.
Grid reference: 501761.

Start from the car park on Southwold Common just east of the water tower. Take the wide path going in a westerly direction with the tower on the left, passing tennis courts and a golf club house, continuing on the path between gorse bushes as far as a large gate and footpath sign. Turn left at this junction on to a metalled track going south towards the river Blyth, with a sight of Walberswick church in the distance. Cross the river by the footbridge and continue along the main path to the Blythburgh to Walberswick road. Turn right and walk along the road to the church. Almost opposite is a lane with a telephone box on the corner. Turn left into the lane, cross another road and pass some houses, then at the end curve of the lane take a wide path on the right going towards Walberswick Common. After reaching a small gate and stile take the path that goes half-right and then down the slope to the marshes. (Ignore the path going west.)

Follow the path through the marshes to join another path by the side of water. Turn right and go towards an old mill, reaching it over a bridge and stile. Turn left at the mill and go over another stile, ignoring a path on the right about 50 yards ahead. Keep on the path with water on the left and Sizewell power station ahead in the distance. Take the next footpath on the right and follow it round a mound to a sign reading 'Private — FP to Dunwich' at the base of a hill on which there is a red-brick building. Take the path to the left, then right, and pass a cottage to join a main path which leads into a lane. Pass through a gate and continue for about 1½ miles to reach the road near Dunwich church. At the church turn left through the village street, passing the Ship public house. Where the road turns sharp right, turn left towards the beach and car park. (In summer it is possible to purchase refreshments here.)

Return by the seashore for about 1½ miles, before taking a path that turns away from the sea to the old mill. At the mill turn right and continue along the path beside the water to Walberswick. On reaching the village street turn right and walk towards the river, and at the south end of the car park turn left on to a signed path and walk along the riverbank to the bridge. Cross the bridge and immediately turn right along the path to the Harbour inn. Turn left on to a road, and after passing the inn turn right on to a footpath through a garden and over a small bridge. Continue on a path across Southwold marshes, crossing

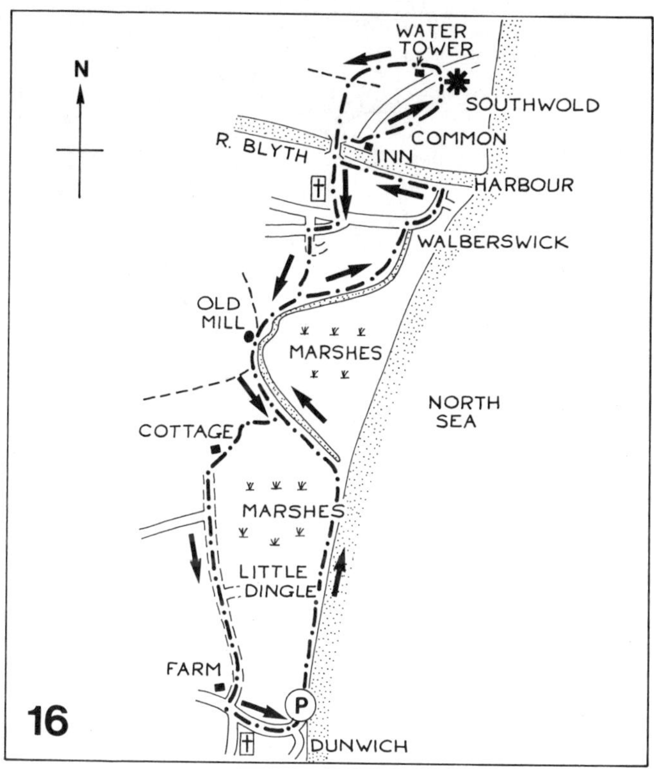

more small bridges to reach the golf course. Carry on to a wide path, then turn left to reach the car park near the water tower.

Harry Chamberlain

17. Wrentham

Distance: about 8½ miles.
Ordnance Survey maps: 1:50,000 sheet 156; 1:25,000 sheets TM47 and TM48.
Grid reference: 499819.

Start at the Five Bells public house at Wrentham, on the B1127 Wrentham to Southwold road. Take the lane on the south side of

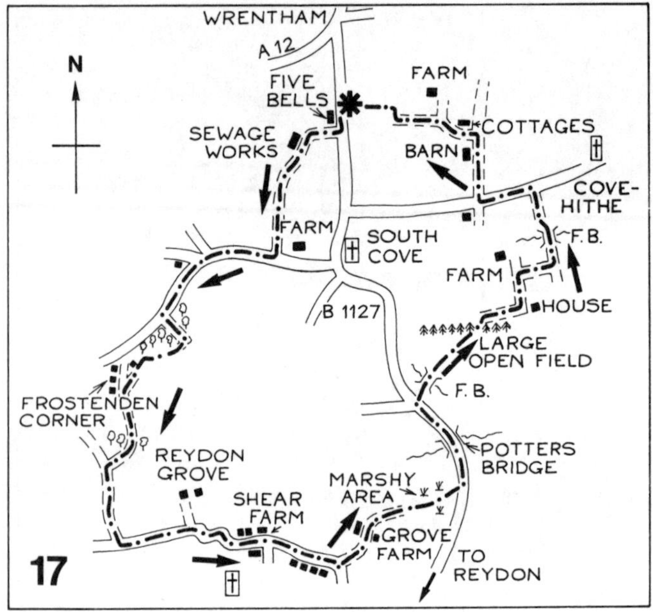

the pub and follow this round a left bend until it ends at a minor road (this lane can be muddy). Turn right along the road to a junction. Ignoring both right forks, continue along the road with eventually a wood on your left, and about 200 yards from the start of the wood take a track on your left. When the track ends, turn right over a stile into a large meadow. Keeping to the right, cross the meadow to another stile on your right. Cross this and turn immediately left over an iron gate and follow the left field edge to another gate leading into a lane. The lane takes you into the small hamlet of Frostenden Corner.

Turn left at the lane junction and follow it round to the left. When it bends right, you continue straight ahead along the track on the left side of a field. Follow this until its junction with a lane, into which turn left, and continue to a junction with a road. Turn left along the road and continue for about 1 mile, ignoring a right fork. Leave the road where it turns sharp right and go along a broad track leading to a farm. Pass through the farmyard and on to a path along the right edge of the field. Follow the field edges until you reach a main road (B1127).

Turn left along the road, over a bridge, and take a path on your right almost opposite a minor road. Follow the path through reeds, over a plank bridge and on to the edge of a large field. Turn right along the field edge and then left until you reach a belt of pines. Pass through these on to a broad track and turn right. Turn left at a house, then sharp right at the next junction. Then at the next junction turn sharp left and continue down to a stream, crossing on a plank bridge (this may require a search in high summer). Over the bridge keep to the left of the rough pasture and enter a lane, which leads to a road. Turn left along the road for about 300 yards and take a lane on your right, past a barn, to some cottages. Turn left in front of these and continue along this lane, ignoring a right turn into a farm. When the lane ends turn right into a field and follow the right field edge back to the road and the Five Bells.

Ann George

18. Carlton Colville

Distance: 13 miles, but may reduced to 10 miles by taking two short cuts.
Ordnance Survey maps: 1:50,000 sheet 156; 1:25,000 sheets TM48 and TM58.
Grid reference: 510894.

This walk starts at the bridleway in Rushmere Road, Carlton Colville, known as Fairhead Loke. Walk along the bridleway for about 1 mile, passing a black barn on your left, and then go through two gates to reach a junction with a footpath. (The footpath straight ahead leads to Mutford church.) Continue along the bridleway, turning north to follow a hedge, and on reaching a road turn left and continue along the road to the bottom of the hill. Here enter a field on the right-hand side and follow a hedge to the edge of a wood; then, turning left in a north-westerly direction, follow the edge of the wood, entering it over a footbridge. Continue in the same direction along the path through the wood to cross a second footbridge, then turn right to follow a hedge to a cottage. Go round the side of a garage and along the driveway to the road. Turn left (south-west) and continue along the road until it turns sharp left. Leave the road and take the signed footpath on the right, following the hedge in a northerly direction to a footbridge. Change to the opposite side of the hedge and continue to Barnby church, passing through the churchyard to the road (A146).

Turn left (south-west) along the road and, immediately after the next junction, turn left in a southerly direction on to a track, with trees on the left and a brick barn on the right, to reach cottages and a road. Turn right and walk along the road in a westerly direction, then leave the road at the next bend and continue in the same direction along a track to another road. Cross the road on to a track following a ditch. Shortly after the track is joined by a path from the right, turn left in a southerly direction to reach a concrete runway, then turn right and continue to a road (B1127). Turn left and walk along the road to a junction with a by-road signposted 'Hill Farm'. Those wishing to shorten the walk should keep straight on along B1127, rejoining the main walk at the next junction. Other walkers follow the road past Hill Farm to a T junction. Looking south from here is a good view over the valley of the river Hundred. Turn left at the junction to rejoin the B1127 and turn right. Those who made the short cut keep straight on, and all walkers then turn right at the next junction to cross the river bridge.

Turn left at the next junction to pass the Hulver Gate public house and turn left into Sandy Lane. After passing the last house, turn right and follow the hedge. Pass through a gate and follow the hedge on its north side. Pass through two more gateways and after the second one turn north-east and follow a hedge, crossing a ditch and a hedge into a pasture. Continue in a north-easterly direction to cross a bridge over a river, then cross a ditch on the left-hand side and carry on to a gate in the north corner of a pasture leading to a track. Go along the track to a junction and then turn east along a track into an arable field. Follow the field edge to the north side and enter the next field at a tree. Go over a rise in the ground to a break in the crop line and follow this to a road. Turn right to Mutford Hall, passing a house and a barn, to leave the farm by a gate on to a track. Follow the track in an easterly direction, keeping the fence on your north side and trees to the south. Cross a metal hurdle and a fence and continue with the fence on your north side through two gates to a lane. Continue to a junction, then turn left through a gate to the end of a field. Turn right on the north side of a hedge and continue to a road.

To shorten the walk, continue along the road past the church and a junction, then turn left on to a bridleway, which joins the bridleway back to Rushmere Road at the black barn mentioned at the start of the walk.

Those doing the full walk should cross the road and go through a gate on the south side to a path. Go through another gate and then turn east to follow a hedge to a gate near a pit, to reach a road. Walk south along the road and at the junction turn left and continue until this road bends right near some cottages. Turn into the track between the cottages and, keeping to the south side of the hedge, follow the track in an easterly direction, pass through a gate, and then, ignoring tracks to right and left, continue in the same direction until the track bears right to pass between houses

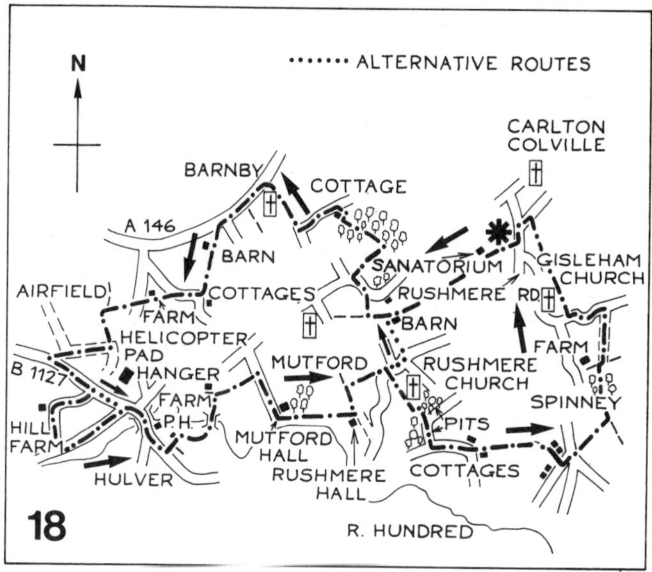

to a road. Turn left and go along the road to the second junction, crossing the road to a stile and path beside a ditch. At a path junction turn left to follow a hedge, crossing to the other side of the hedge at a gap, then continue on through a spinney, passing between trees and a ditch to reach the edge of a field. Turn right on to a track, then turn left to follow the track along a field edge next to a ditch to a road, going left along the road to reach Gisleham church.

Go through the white gate into the churchyard, passing the east end of the church, then through a fence, and follow the hedge, changing sides about 200 yards from the church. Continue to follow the hedge and take the same line through the field where the hedge ends. Go over a stile into a paddock, then over another stile into a road. This is The Street, Carlton Colville, a short distance from the starting point.

John Sayer

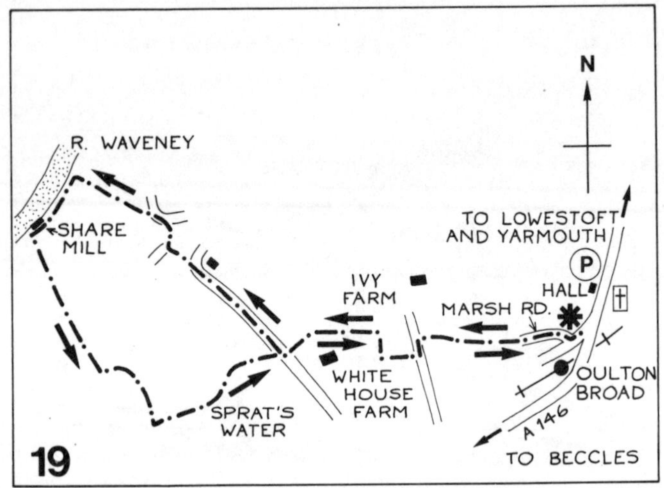

19. Oulton Broad

Distance: 4½ miles.
Ordnance Survey maps: 1:50,000 sheet 134; 1:25,000 sheets TM49 and TM59.
Grid reference: 519921.

Leave A146 at the north end of the railway bridge near Oulton Broad South station and go down Marsh Road (signpost 'Burnt Hill ¾ mile'). At the railway station fork right into a narrow road and continue straight on between holiday chalets and over a stile. A well marked track leads to a path with a caravan park and hedge on the right. Where the path meets a farm lane a few yards along on the left, enter a field over a stile. Go straight across the field and over another stile. Turn right and follow round two sides of a field (with a dyke on the right) until you meet a wide stony lane near a farm.

Turn right and follow the lane across the marshes. Where the track turns sharp right go straight on, through (or over) a gate on to a path across a field to another gate near an old shed, and cross into the next field. Where the track bears left, go diagonally right across the grass towards posts and a gate. Go through the gate and turn left along a wide track with a dyke on the left and crops on the right until the track swings right. Continue straight on with the dyke on the left along the edge of a field until you reach the bank of the river Waveney.

Turn left on to the riverbank and continue until you reach some buildings (the Share Mill). Leave the river wall over a footbridge and walk between two dykes on a wide path until you reach some trees and a sign 'Sprat's Water'. Turn left and follow a grassy path with a dyke on the right until you come to a field with dead trees. Look straight across to a gate on to a lane. You have rejoined your outward route and can follow it back to your starting point.

Margaret Mooney

Index

Aldham Mill 35
Ampton Racecourse 15
Barking 32
Barnby 59
Barton Mills 10,11
Blyth, river 56
Bobby Hill 43
Bradfield St Clare 19
Bradfield St George 16
Brett, river 34, 35, 36
Brockley Green 21
Carlton Colville 59, 61
Cavenham Heath 11
Chelmondiston 37, 39
Cherry Hill 10, 11
Cordell Hall 23
Culford 14
Dagworth 29
Dalham 6
Darmsden 31
Deben, river 45
Dedham Mill 37
Dunwich 56
Erwarton 39
Fornham St Martin 12, 16
Framlingham 47, 53
Frostenden Corner 58
Gazeley 5
Gipping, river 29, 30
Gisleham 61
Glemsford 26
Grundle 40
Hadleigh 34
Hawkedon 20, 24
Hengrave Bridge 14
Hepworth 43
Herringswell 9
Hessett 18
Higham 35, 36
Hulver Gate 60
Hundred, river 60
Ingham 15
Kennett, river 4, 6
Kentwell Hall 25
Kersey 32, 35
Kingshall Street 18
Kyson Point 45
Langham 37
Lark, river 8, 10, 12, 13
Leiston 53
Long Melford 24, 27
Martlesham Creek 45
Mildenhall 7, 10, 12
Monks Park Wood 19
Moulton 4, 7
Mutford Hall 60
Needham Market 30, 32
North Green 50, 51, 52
Ore, river 48
Orwell, river 37
Oulton Broad 62
Parham 50-1
Pin Mill 39
Priestley Woods 32
Purton Green 23
Rede 22
Red Lodge 8
Rougham 18
St Clare Hall 19
Scotchford Bridge 26
Seckford Hall 46
Shotley Hall 37
Silverlace Green 51
Sizewell 54
Somerton 20
Southwold 56
Squirrel's Hall 42
Stansfield 24
Stanstead 26
Stanton 39, 44
Stour, river 36, 37
Stowmarket 28, 30
Stowupland 29
Stratford St Mary 35, 37
Temple Bridge 11
Timworth 16
Toppesfield Bridge 34
Tuddenham 10, 11
Walberswick 56
Walsham le Willows 41, 42
Wamil Hall 8
Wattisfield 42, 43
Waveney, river 63
West Stow 14
Woodbridge 44, 45, 46
Wordwell 15
Worlington 8
Wrentham 57, 59